TRANSFORMING THE REBOUND INTO RECOVERY

EAST ASIA AND PACIFIC UPDATE **NOVEMBER 2009**

TRANSFORMING THE REBOUND INTO RECOVERY

A WORLD BANK ECONOMIC UPDATE FOR THE EAST ASIA AND PACIFIC REGION

THE WORLD BANK

1818 H Street NW
Washington DC 20433
Telephone: 202-473-1000
Internet: www.worldbank.org
E-mail: feedback@worldbank.org

1 2 3 4 12 11 10 9

ISBN: 978-0-8213-8267-7
DOI: 10.1596/978-0-8213-8267-7

CONTENTS

ACKNOWLEDGMENTS

The *East Asia and Pacific Update* was prepared by Ivailo Izvorski (iizvorski@worldbank.org) and Antonio Ollero under the guidance of Vikram Nehru (East Asia and Pacific Regional Chief Economist and Director, Department for Poverty Reduction, Economic Management, Private and Financial Sector Development). Inputs were provided by country economists and analysts across World Bank offices in East Asia and the Pacific, and by Andrew Burns, Ratchada Anantavrasilpa, Kirida Bhaopichitr, Eric Le Borgne, Mansoor Dailami, Sung-Soo Eun, Xu Gao, Sepideh Khazai, Ulrich Lachler, Sheryll Namingit, Mick Riordan, Frederico Gil Sander, Philip Schellekens, Manohar Sharma, Ashley Taylor, Hans Timmer, Ekaterina Vostroknutova, and Xiao Ye. The update has benefitted from the assistance and guidance on design and external communications by Mohamad Al-Arief and the External Affairs Team, and from assistance by Lynn Gross.

Emerging East Asia as used in this report includes Developing East Asia (China, Indonesia, Malaysia, Philippines, Thailand, Cambodia, Lao PDR, Mongolia, Papua New Guinea, Timor-Leste, Vietnam, and the island economies in the Pacific) and the Newly Industrialized Economies (NIEs). The NIEs include Hong Kong, China; the Republic of Korea; Singapore; and Taiwan, China. Middle-income countries, as used in this report, refer to China, Indonesia, Malaysia, and Thailand. Low-income countries as used in this report include Cambodia, Lao PDR, and Vietnam. The ASEAN member countries are Brunei Darussalam, Cambodia, Indonesia, Lao PDR, Malaysia, Myanmar, Philippines, Singapore, Thailand, and Vietnam. ASEAN+3 refers to all members of ASEAN plus China, Korea, and Japan, and ASEAN+6 also includes Australia, India, and New Zealand.

www.worldbank.org/eapupdate

SUMMARY

East Asia's rebound from the economic downturn has been surprisingly swift and very welcome. A year ago, exports and industrial production fell sharply across the region, layoffs were on the rise, and capital flowed out weakening asset prices and currencies. A vigorous and timely fiscal and monetary stimulus in most countries in East Asia, led by China and the Republic of Korea, along with decisive measures in developed economies to prevent a financial meltdown after the collapse of Lehman Brothers, have stopped the decline in activity and set in motion the regional rebound. The shift to inventory restocking since mid-2009 has also helped boost growth. These factors have led us to revise our projection for real GDP growth in developing East Asia up by 1.3 percentage points since the previous forecast in April. All in all, real GDP growth is set to slow to 6.7 percent in 2009 from 8 percent in 2008, or much more moderately than after the 1997-98 Asian financial crisis.

Developments in East Asia remain strongly influenced by China. Take China out of the equation, and the rest of the region is recovering with less vigor. For 2009 as a whole, output is projected to contract in Cambodia, Malaysia and Thailand and barely grow in Mongolia and some of the Pacific islands. Even with solid growth in Indonesia and Vietnam, developing East Asia excluding China is projected to grow more slowly in 2009 than South Asia, the Middle East and North Africa, and only modestly faster than Sub-Saharan Africa.

The aggregate numbers mask not only large differences in growth performance: they tell an incomplete story about the social and poverty impact of the crisis. Lack of high frequency data on household incomes and expenditures makes it difficult to track how the poor are faring. Based on past patterns of poverty and growth – which may not hold during the current downturn and rebound – an additional 14 million people will remain in poverty in the region in 2010 as a result of this crisis. Reduced demand for labor during the downturn typically meant reduced work hours or lower wages, rather than outright layoffs. In some countries, where layoffs occurred, workers moved to the informal sector. In the end, labor incomes fell substantially in 2009, with adverse consequences for living standards. Poverty estimates do not capture these adverse consequences.

The rebound has yet to become a recovery. That is why the authorities in the region are mindful of the risks of a premature withdrawal of stimulus, given the large output gaps and concerns that developed countries are converging to a slower-growth equilibrium. Some governments in the region will have the fiscal space to sustain fiscal stimulus until recovery is on a firmer footing and private investment has been restarted. Others will be more restrained because of limited fiscal space. Overall, governments are aware that fiscal and monetary stimulus alone cannot sustain domestic demand for an extended period of time, especially if investors are not reassured that the authorities will have viable exit strategies in place and will bring government debt to levels that will not jeopardize long-term debt sustainability. There are limits, moreover, to what fiscal and monetary policies can accomplish if recovery in the developed countries, notably the U.S., remains weak for a longer period than currently deemed likely.

The crisis has prompted countries in the region to rethink their development strategies. For most, the choice between growth driven by exports, on the one hand, and growth driven by domestic demand, on the other, is a false one. Countries need to resist protectionism, remain open and become more, not less, integrated into the global economy to continue to reap the benefits of global knowledge, technologies and innovation. At the same time, governments are realizing that more growth can be extracted from domestic demand if they ease or eliminate incentives that favor the quick buildup of export-led, investment-heavy manufacturing supported by undervalued exchange rates and suppressed domestic consumption and services. Some governments are rethinking how to manage risks stemming from large and volatile capital inflows, especially given concerns about new asset price bubbles.

The regional outlook for consolidation of the rebound into recovery and a return to rapid growth confronts downside and upside risks. Downside risks include a double dip in economic activity in the advanced countries as stimulus measures and inventory restocking wear off. This will challenge many East Asian countries that have little fiscal space to continue to finance fiscal stimulus programs without external assistance. But they will be assisted by China that has the resources to maintain its current fiscal stance for several years if necessary. There will be limits to China's capacity for further monetary stimulus, however, following the surge in credit by 30 percent of GDP in 2009. On the upside, a more robust recovery in the advanced countries could remove some of the imperative for rebalancing in developing East Asia and encourage sustaining the pre-crisis export-oriented growth model. The upside also carries with it the risk of larger capital inflows causing new asset price bubbles and complicating macroeconomic policies. Managing both risks will be a challenge that will require measures to rebalance growth while advancing integration with global markets and retooling institutions to encourage innovation.

Over the medium term, can developing East Asia sustain rapid growth, even if the rest of the world grows slowly? This will depend on whether East Asia can integrate further regionally – through better facilitation of trade in goods and by extending its liberal trade policies to services. Moving up the value-added chain in global production networks will present an additional impetus to growth, as the benefits of new technology and innovation spread more broadly through the countries in the region. The service sector holds enormous potential for East Asia. Measures to spur competition in the service sector, combined with policies to ease restrictions to internal migration and trade, bolster education and improve the environment for private investment and innovation, will allow countries to take a fuller advantage of the benefits of agglomeration, and create more favorable conditions for the emergence of innovative global companies.

ABBREVIATIONS

ADB	Asian Development Bank
ASEAN	Association of Southeast Asian Nations (Brunei Darusalam, Cambodia, Indonesia, Lao PDR, Malaysia, Myanmar, Philippines, Singapore, Thailand, and Vietnam)
BEA	U.S. Bureau of Economic Analysis
BPO	Business Process Outsourcing
CIC	China Investment Corporation
CMI	Chiang Mai Initiative
EBRD	European Bank for Reconstruction and Development
ECB	European Central Bank
EIB	European Investment Bank
EU	European Union
FDI	Foreign Direct Investment
G20	Group of Twenty
G-3	The United States, the Eurozone, and Japan
GDP	Gross Domestic Product
IMF	International Monetary Fund
IPO	Initial Public Offering
LCD	Liquid Crystal Display
NA	National Accounts
NIEs	Newly Industrialized Economies (Hong Kong, China; Korea; Singapore; and Taiwan, China)
NPLs	Nonperforming Loans
OECD	Organisation for Economic Co-operation and Development
OPEC	Organization of Petroleum Exporting Countries
PMI	Purchasing Managers Index
PNG	Papua New Guinea
RMB	Chinese renminbi
SAR	Special Administrative Region
SITC	Standard Industrial Trade Classification
SMEs	Small and Medium Enterprises
U.S.	United States

Countries

CHN	China
HKG	Hong Kong, China
IDN	Indonesia
KHM	Cambodia
KOR	Korea, Rep. of
LAO	Lao PDR
MNG	Mongolia
MYS	Malaysia
PHL	Philippines
SGP	Singapore
THA	Thailand
TWN	Taiwan, China
VNM	Vietnam

I. THE REBOUND

EAST ASIA IS LEADING THE GLOBAL REBOUND

A vigorous economic rebound is under way in East Asia since the second quarter of 2009, following the sharp impact from the financial crisis and the global recession that began in late 2008. As much as the reduction in exports and industrial production across the region in the fourth quarter of 2008 and the first quarter of 2009 was unexpectedly swift and deep, so is the strength of the rebound, with doubts about green shoots dispelled in a matter of months and replaced by near-consensus views of a synchronized global rebound led by emerging East Asia. The robust rebound is due to a combination of timely and large fiscal and monetary stimulus in most countries in East Asia, notably in China, and a powerful process of inventory restocking that began after mid-2009. Globally, the advanced economies joined the rebound trend in the third quarter of 2009, and their contributions to global industrial production – notably driven by inventory accumulation – have begun to outpace the contribution from the East Asia region. These developments are set against a background of solid macroeconomic fundamentals, including high foreign exchange reserves, large private and corporate savings, and low corporate and government debt. The region's well-capitalized banks and much improved banking supervision since the 1997-98 Asian financial crisis have also helped limit financial contagion and the transmission of the forces of global recession.

Figure 1. Real GDP growth in East Asia slowed by less than during the 1997-98 crisis

(Percent change year-on-year)

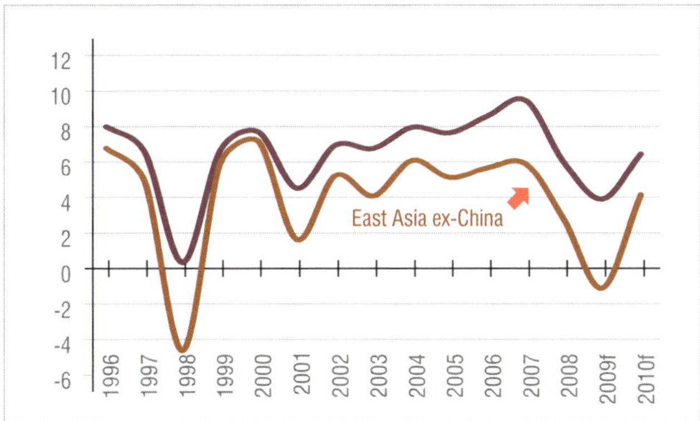

Sources: Datastream and World Bank staff calculations.

Figure 2. Those that fell are not fully up:

(Percent change in real GDP, seasonally adjusted not annualized)

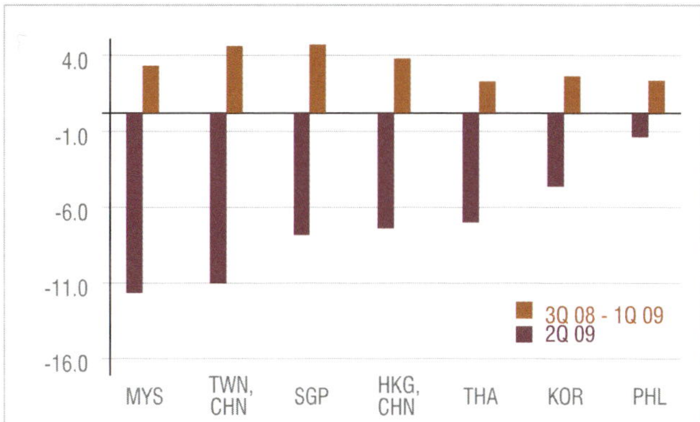

Sources: Datastream and World Bank staff calculations.

The global economic recession has been the worst since World War II, and the financial crisis the most severe since the Great Depression, but East Asia's real GDP growth did better than during the 1997-98 Asian financial crisis. In fact, growth in 2009 is set to slow to a pace only slightly lower than during the 2001 "dot com" U.S. recession which represented a pure external demand shock to East Asia and during which China, similarly to the current crisis, implemented a large fiscal stimulus package (Figure 1).[1] Four East Asian economies fell into recession during the current global crisis, and all four emerged from it in the second quarter of 2009 (Thailand, Malaysia, Singapore and Taiwan, China).

The rebound so far has been strong but it has yet to offset fully the earlier decline (Figure 2). China - and Indonesia and Vietnam - are the exceptions, without a single quarter of negative growth. The rapid increase in China's real GDP and its components has helped the regional and global rebound, but there are limits to the extent China can replace weak final demand in the U.S., the EU and Japan (the G-3) given that the size of its economy is equivalent to a tenth of theirs combined. Yet China's contribution

1 For details of the Chinese stimulus package implemented during 1998-2002, see the April 2009 EAP Update, "Battling the Forces of the Global Recession."

Figure 3. China's global economic position has expanded considerably

(Change year-on-year in billions of U.S. dollars, 2008)

The increase in China's **GDP** was larger than that of the G-3 during the crisis, up from a third before 2008

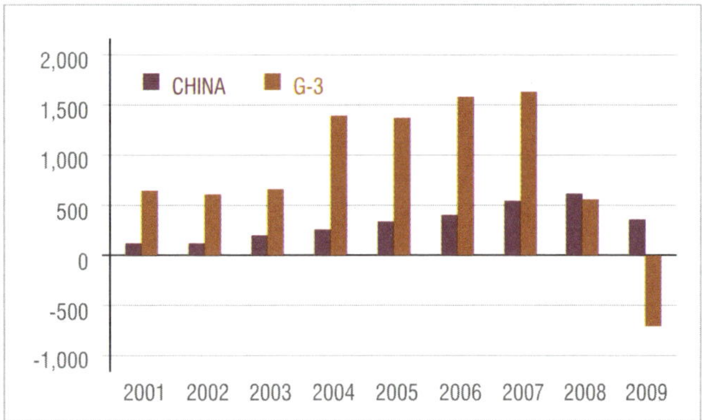

The increment in **domestic demand** has also been larger than the G-3 during the crisis, thanks to government-influenced investment

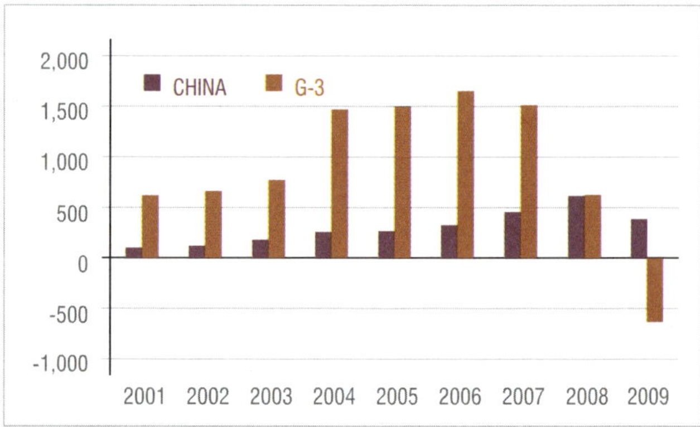

Private consumption was much more subdued, except in 2009

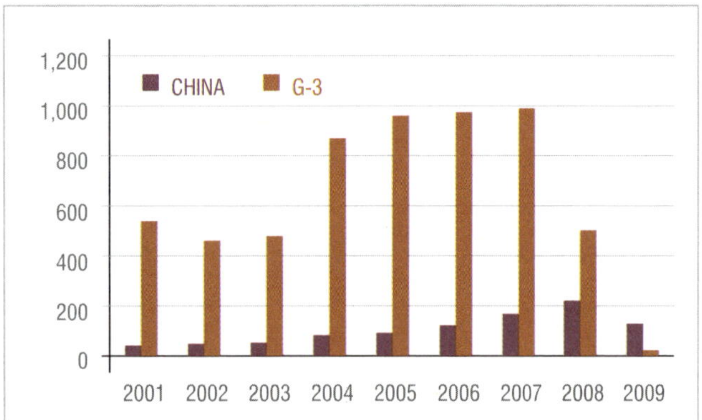

And China's incremental **imports** fell by less than the G-3 in 2009 as a whole

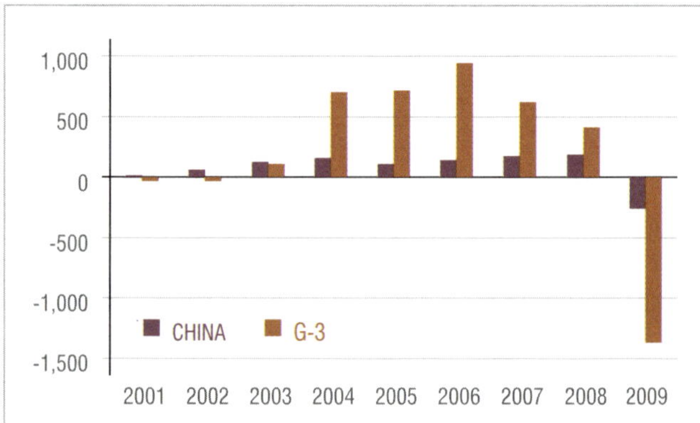

China was instrumental in the revival of global industrial production, but the contribution from high income countries rose much more in the third quarter (contribution to global growth, percentage points, quarter-on-quarter)

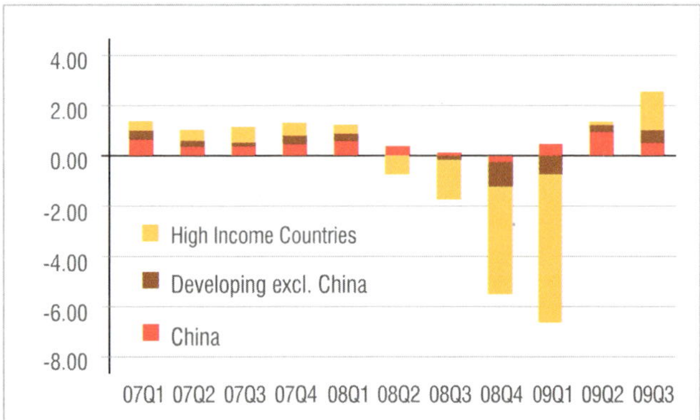

Sources: Haver, Eurostat and World Bank staff calculations.

has been rising over the years and its incremental private consumption, domestic demand and imports of goods and services exceeded that of the U.S. and Japan individually in 2008, and almost certainly in 2009 given the recession in those two countries (Figure 3). Rebalancing growth in China should help extract more growth from domestic demand and should help boost further its influence on the region and the world (see below).

INDUSTRIAL PRODUCTION LED THE DECLINE AND NOW THE REBOUND

Inventory restocking, fiscal stimulus and signs of increasing final demand in China are helping drive a strong recovery in industrial production across the region following the sharp contraction in late 2008 and early 2009 (Figure 4). Both

Figure 4. Industrial production in East Asia is recovering swiftly

(In percent, year-on-year)

Sources: Datastream and World Bank staff calculations.

Figure 5. Purchasing managers indices have also rebounded

(Index, 2007-2009)

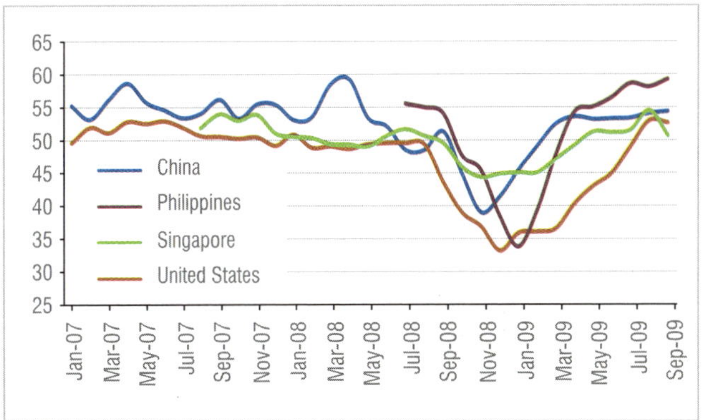

Sources: Datastream and World Bank staff calculations.

growth rates and output levels are recovering in a V-shaped fashion, ahead of the rebound in the advanced economies. The Purchasing Managers' Index (PMI) – a measure of business confidence in the expansion of production, sales and employment – has also rebounded sharply, with almost all components, including domestic and export orders, and employment, suggesting expansion (Figure 5). The recovery, much like the preceding decline, has been most pronounced in more open countries or in countries with a larger share of high-technology manufacturing in exports. Of course, high-technology does not mean high value-added, which is why sharp declines in production and activity translated into smaller impacts on GDP.

The recovery in industrial production has been swift, but there is substantial heterogeneity across the region and, on average, production levels are still 10 percent down from the pre-crisis peak. For China, the Republic of Korea, and Indonesia, the recovery in production has been faster than the 21 months it took for regional output to reach the pre-crisis peak after the 1997-98 Asian financial crisis. The large fiscal and monetary stimulus packages in China and Korea have been the key factors underpinning the rebound, in China's case also supporting a larger increase in domestic demand that has drawn imports of electronics, electrical appliances, and capital goods, including from Korea (Figure 6). Tax breaks on automobile sales in China and Korea, together with subsidies for trading in older vehicles, have also contributed to the surge in sales and production. In December 2008, for the first time ever, vehicle sales in China surpassed those in the U.S., making China the largest automotive market in the world (Figure 7). Thailand's production is also close to its pre-crisis peak, even though capacity utilization is below the levels that prevailed

Figure 6. Levels of industrial production are still below the pre-crisis peak in most countries */

(Index, recent peak = 100 and months since recent peak)

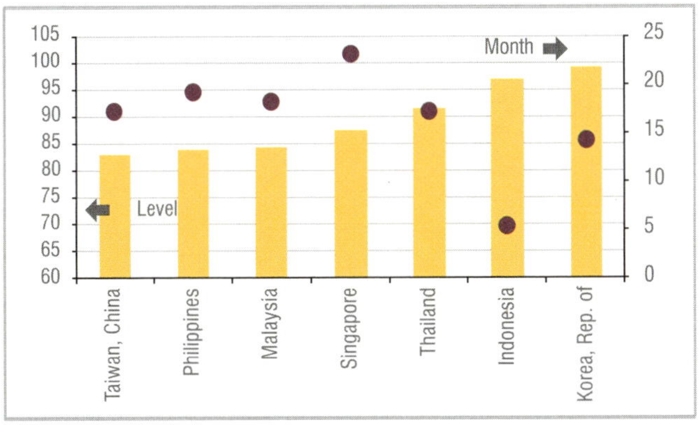

Sources: Datastream and World Bank staff calculations.
*/Bars (left hand side): level of industrial production relative to the recent peak; dots (right hand side): number of months since the recent peak.

Figure 7. Vehicle sales in China have surpassed those in the U.S.

(In thousands, Jan'2005-Aug'2009)

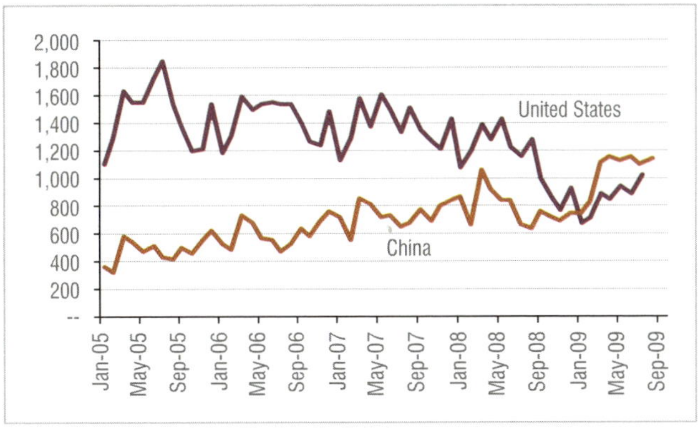

Sources: Datastream and World Bank staff calculations.

Figure 8. Capacity utilization is recovering

(In percent, Jan'2007-Jul'2009)

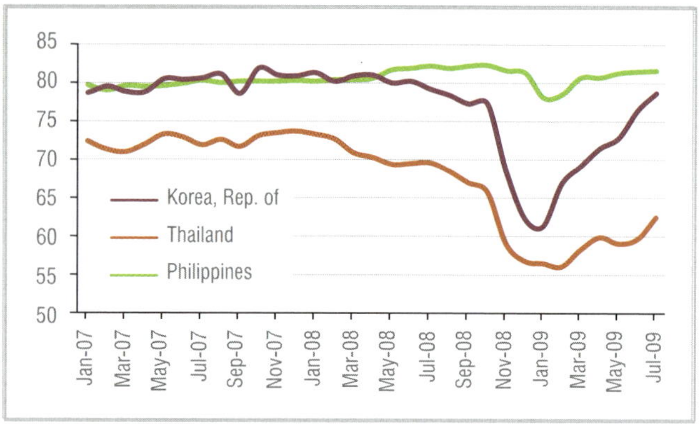

Sources: CEIC and World Bank staff calculations.

Figure 9. Korea's Hyundai has increased its share in the U.S. during the crisis

(In percent of total automotive market)

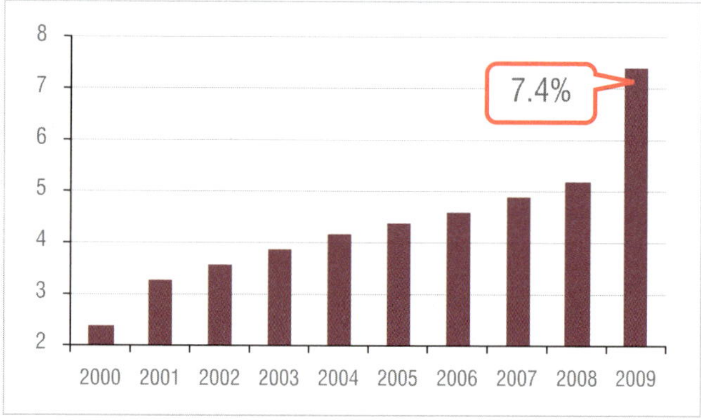

Source: Autodata through *Fortune* magazine.

through the middle of last year (Figure 8). But output levels in other countries in the region, including Singapore and Taiwan, China, are still 15 percent below peaks reached 18 months earlier, trailing the pace at which recovery progressed after the 1997-98 Asian financial crisis.

EXPORTS HAVE ALSO REBOUNDED STRONGLY

Exports have bounced back from the lows reached in early 2009 as companies abroad began restocking depleted inventories and final demand within the region started picking up. But overall export levels are still a fifth lower than in 2008 because of depressed demand in developed countries. In seasonally adjusted terms, exports are up 40 percent from the trough reached in January-February 2009, following a 45 percent contraction from the pre-crisis peak in July 2008 (Figure 10 and Figure 11). Korea has led the recovery with a 65 percent surge in exports, benefitting from increased demand in China for consumer electronics and automobiles, and the ability of several Korean firms, notably car manufacturer Hyundai/Kia, to gain market share in the U.S. despite the recession there (Figure 9). China's shipments abroad have also stabilized and begun to rise, but the 35 percent increase from the February 2009 trough has yet to offset the 55 percent contraction from the peak in mid-2008 given China's dependence on final demand in developed economies.

Figure 10. Exports have rebounded, but levels are still substantially down

(Percent change from trough; "t" denotes the dates in the column)

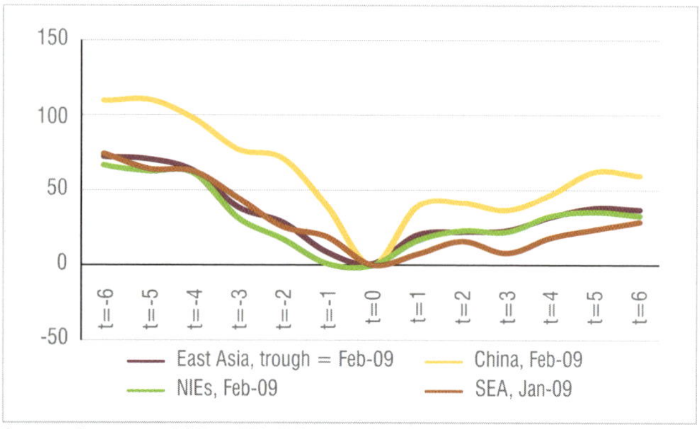

Sources: Datastream, CEIC and World Bank staff calculations.

Figure 11. The ratio of exports to GDP has risen only in Korea

(Exports in percent of GDP)

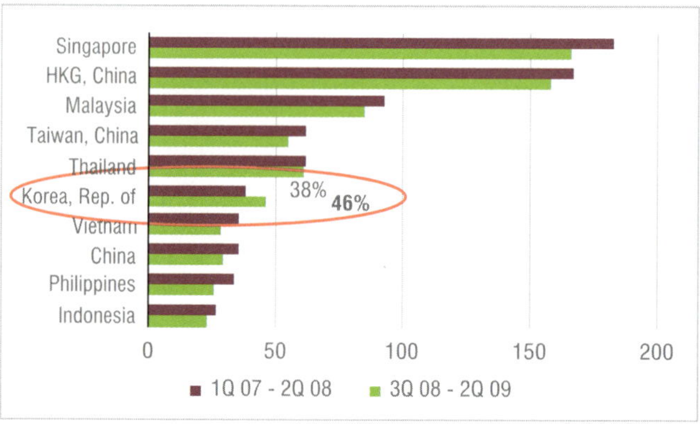

Sources: Datastream, CEIC and World Bank staff calculations.

Figure 12. Korea's companies gained global market share as others in Asia stumbled

(In percent of world exports)

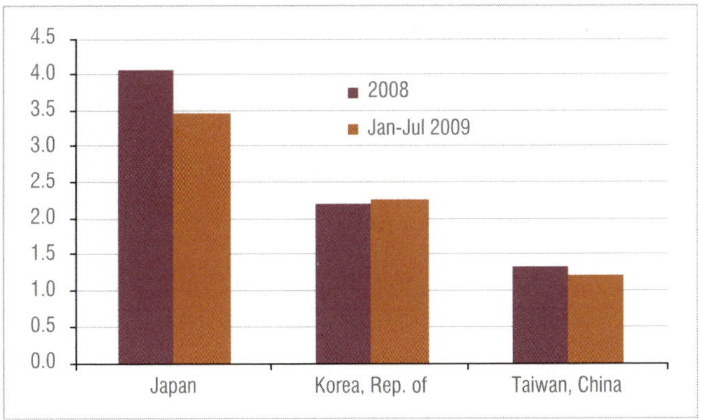

Sources: Datastream, CEIC and World Bank staff calculations.

Figure 13. China has overtaken Germany as the world's largest exporter

(In billions of U.S. dollars)

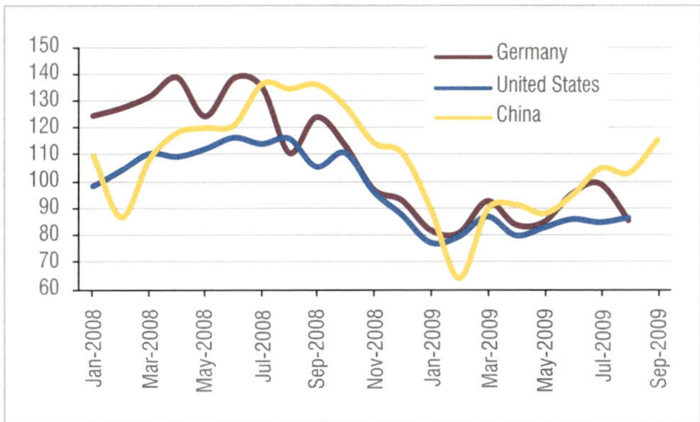

Sources: Datastream, CEIC and World Bank staff calculations.

The initial contraction in exports represented a more powerful drag on real GDP growth in countries with larger export sectors, higher domestic value-added for shipments abroad, and higher share of advanced manufacturing in exports. Real GDP fell most in Thailand and Malaysia among the region's middle-income countries, in large part because of these factors, notably the higher value-added component of their electronics and automobile industries (notably in the case of Thailand).

As a result of the crisis, exports now account for a lower share of GDP in all countries in East Asia except Korea. Exports of goods and services in Korea rose from 38 percent of GDP in the year ending with the second quarter of 2008 to 46 percent in the year starting with the third quarter of 2008 (Figure 11). This outcome reflects in large part the ability of Korean firms to gain market share against key competitors from Japan and Taiwan, China during the recession, including in export sectors with high-value added and high likelihood of strong recovery such as memory chips, mobile phones, and LCD panels.[2] China, meanwhile, overtook Germany as the world's top exporting country starting in April (Figure 13).

China has been a key factor in East Asia's and the world's foreign trade rebound this year. Although China's imports are set to fall for 2009 as a whole, they are projected to decline by much less than the G-3 combined (last panel, Figure 3). Moreover, China's imports fell by less than the imports of any of the G-3 in the first quarter and rebounded more sharply in the second quarter, as measured both in percentage terms and in U.S. dollars (Figure 14). There are two channels by which China has helped lift East Asian export performance. First, as companies began replenishing depleted inventories, those based in China as part of global supply chains restocked parts and components used for the assembly of electronics products bound primarily for the G-3. Secondly, final demand in China has risen robustly this year, supported by expansive fiscal and monetary policy, benefitting both imports of consumer

Figure 14. China's imports have rebounded more strongly than those of the G-3

(In billions of U.S. dollars)

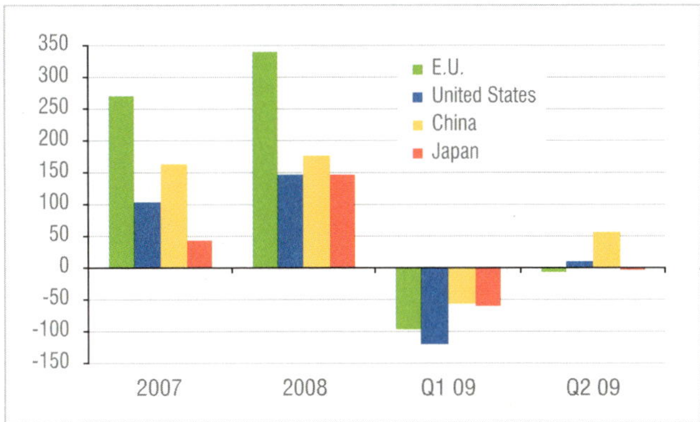

Sources: Datastream, CEIC and World Bank staff calculations.

2 Korean semiconductor manufacturers Samsung Electronics and Hynix Semiconductor expanded their share of the global (DRAM) market from 53.1 percent in the second quarter of 2008 to 61 percent in the second quarter of 2009. Korean LCD manufacturers, led by Samsung and LG Display, solidified their control of the global flat-screen display market with shares rising from 45.5 percent to 49.4 percent. Mobile phone makers Samsung Electronics and LG Electronics strengthened their position in the global mobile phone market with shares up from 24.7 percent to 30.6 percent share as the relative positions of key rivals Nokia, Motorola and Sony Ericsson weakened.

Figure 15. Final goods dominate China's exports to the G-3

(In percent of total exports)

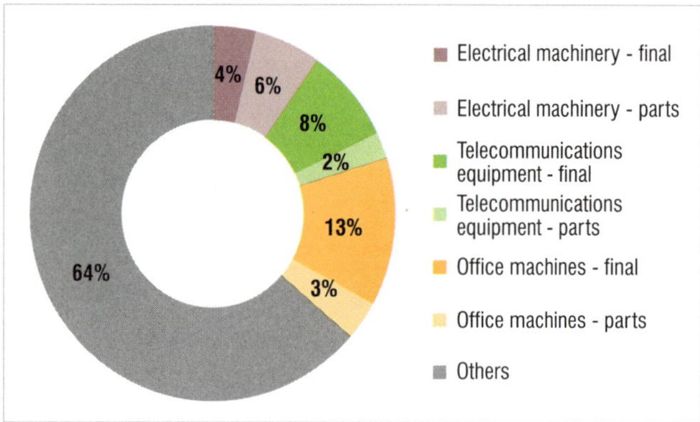

Sources: Datastream, CEIC and World Bank staff calculations.

Figure 16. Parts and components dominate China's imports from East Asia

(In percent of total exports)

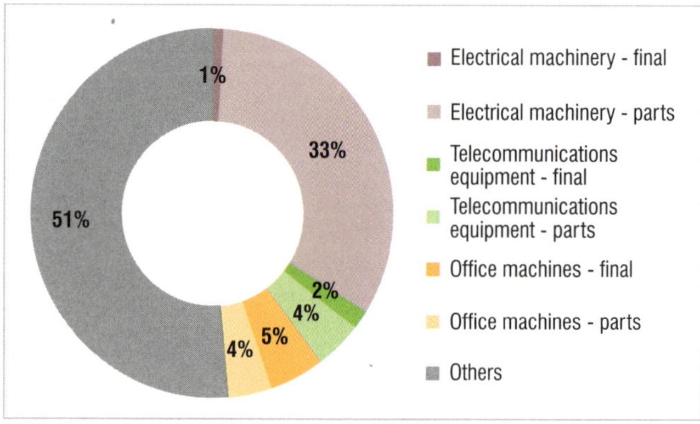

Sources: Datastream, CEIC and World Bank staff calculations.

Figure 17. Parts and components dominate exports to China for all countries but Malaysia

(In percent of total exports, 2008)

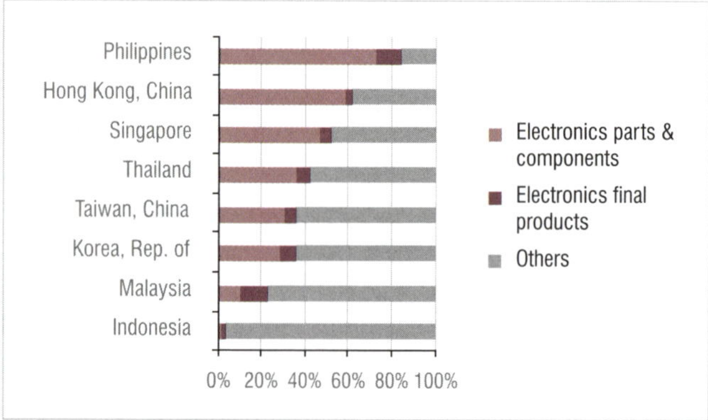

Sources: Datastream, CEIC and World Bank staff calculations.

durables, notably from Korea and Taiwan, China, and raw materials used in construction activities. Part of the surge in imports of raw materials reflects strategic stock-piling by state-owned companies taking advantage of what they perceive to be low prices.

Trade in electronics exemplifies China's role as an increasingly important conduit of growth between the G-3 and the rest of East Asia. Electronics products comprise a significant share of China's exports to the G-3 (36 percent) and China's imports from East Asia (49 percent).[3] China's electronics exports to the G-3, however, consist predominantly of equipment and devices (with final goods amounting to 68 percent of the total and parts for the rest), while electronics imports from East Asia are primarily parts and components with 85 percent of the total (Figure 15 through Figure 17). Until final demand for electronics in the G-3 recovers, production and exports from East Asia of electronic parts and components to China will remain subdued even if the surge in domestic demand in China is sustained.

China's infrastructure-focused fiscal stimulus, combined with the surge in the country's automobile production and strategic stocking of raw materials, has boosted commodity imports and contributed to the recovery of regional exports.[4] China's imports of copper were three times the average for 2007 and 2008 in June, and purchases of primary aluminum were also much higher (Figure 18). Normally a net exporter of steel, China became a net importer this year even as its mills boosted production to 90 percent of capacity. Although East Asia's mines and mills are not the largest suppliers of metals to China, they have substantial positions that have been strengthened during the crisis. For some countries in the region, metals comprise a sizable share of total exports. For example, almost all of Mongolia's exports of copper and iron are to China. These exports, in turn, account for two-thirds of Mongolia's overall shipments abroad and strongly affect the country's economic activity (Figure 19).

3 In the discussion, electronic products are defined to consist of: (1) electrical machinery, apparatus and appliances (SITC 77); (2) telecommunications and sound recording apparatus (SITC 76) and, (3) office machines and automatic data processing equipment (SITC 75).

4 China is the world's largest consumer of crude steel (34 percent of global consumption), copper (28 percent), and aluminum (33 percent). But China is also the world's largest producer and exporter of these metals.

Figure 18. China's imports of metal ore have surged

(In billions of U.S. dollars)

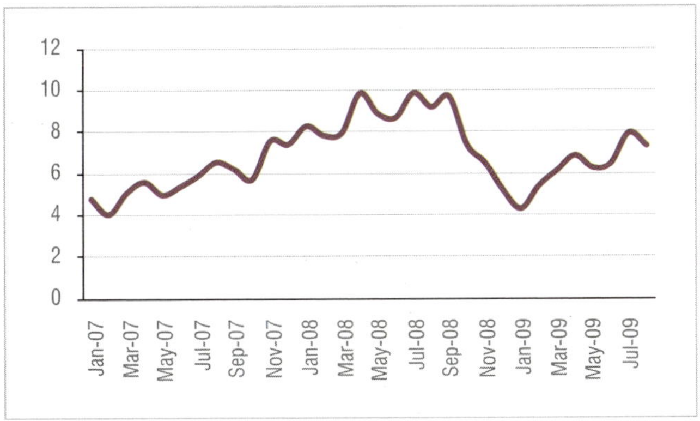

Sources: Datastream, CEIC and World Bank staff calculations.

Figure 19. Metals account for a large share of exports for some countries in the region

(In percent of total exports, excludes gold)

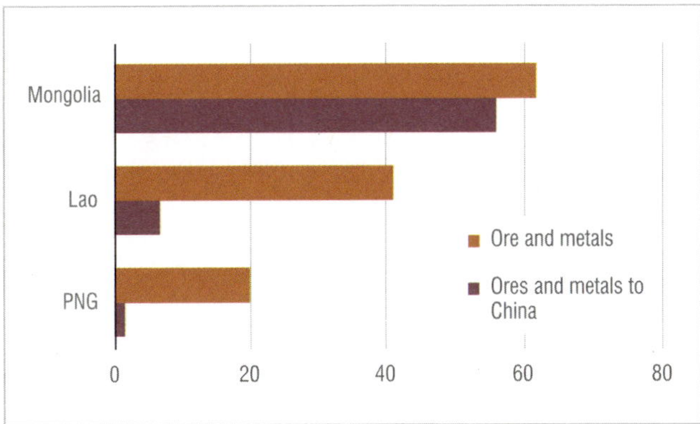

Sources: Datastream, CEIC and World Bank staff calculations.

China has provided a larger boost to the rebound in regional exports than the rest of the world thus far. This is the conclusion both at the aggregate level and at the disaggregated level, including the broad range of commodities and manufactures other than electronics – fifteen products, defined at the two-digit SITC level that account for 70 percent of non-electronics trade (Figure 20). Such an outcome cannot be sustained for an extended period of time, given that the rest of the world ultimately accounts for two-thirds of regional exports that are increasingly intermediated through Chinese companies.

Figure 20. China has been a stronger driver of the regional export rebound this year than the rest of the world

(Index, U.S. dollar values of exports, June-2008=100)

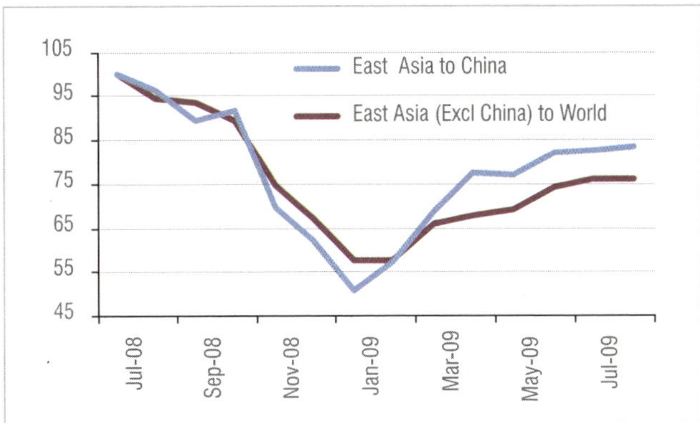

Sources: Datastream, CEIC and World Bank staff calculations.

Demand by China has raced ahead of global demand and demand by the G3 has lagged. Imports by the EU, the U.S. and Japan each fell more steeply than world imports during this global recession and they have recovered less sharply so far. Weak demand by the G-3, the market for 47 percent of China's exports and nearly two-thirds of the shipments abroad by East Asia, is reflected in China's trade numbers: after electronics, China's largest exports to the G-3 are consumer products (including textiles and footwear) and durables (including furniture) that have shrunk in line with weak consumer spending in the advanced economies. The other countries in the region have similarly suffered from weak G3 demand.

CAPITAL INFLOWS ARE RECOVERING

Renewed nonresident purchases of government debt, combined with repatriation of assets by local investors, shifted large capital outflows in the second half of 2008 into robust inflows during the first half of 2009, notably since March (Table 1). Resident capital reflows in the first half were the largest this decade, reflecting expectations that returns on East Asian assets will outperform those on foreign securities, especially factoring in potential currency appreciation. Such reflows are raising concerns about asset price bubbles, however, and prompting the authorities to rethink policies to address large and volatile investment flows.

Nonresidents have boosted purchases of government debt as well, facilitated by a surge in new issuance (Figure 21). Gross foreign and domestic bond issuance in East Asia amounted to $19 billion thus far this year, two and a half times the average of the last two

Table 1. Capital inflows are recovering

(In billions of U.S. dollars)

	2007			2008			2009
	H1	H2	Total	H1	H2	Total	H1
Net capital flows	**80**	**59**	**140**	**98**	**-99**	**-1**	**44**
Current account balance	236	254	489	253	484	737	238
Merchandise balance	206	225	431	184	402	587	206
Invisibles balance	30	29	59	69	82	151	32
Capital and financial account	64	37	101	86	-75	11	54
of which:							
FDI net	57	37	93	39	102	141	18
Portfolio	-30	-22	-52	-31	-37	-68	-1
Equity	-29	-86	-116	-46	-13	-58	-7
Debt	-1	65	64	14	-25	-11	5
Other investment	116	208	324	153	-51	102	-71
Resident lending abroad	-103	-175	-277	-74	-94	-167	104
Errors and omissions	17	22	39	12	-25	-13	-11
Reserves (-=increase)	-316	-313	-629	-351	-385	-736	-282

Sources: National authorities and Bank staff projections.

Figure 21. Bond issuance has surged this year, but new IPOs and syndicated bank loans remain weak

(In billions of U.S. dollars)

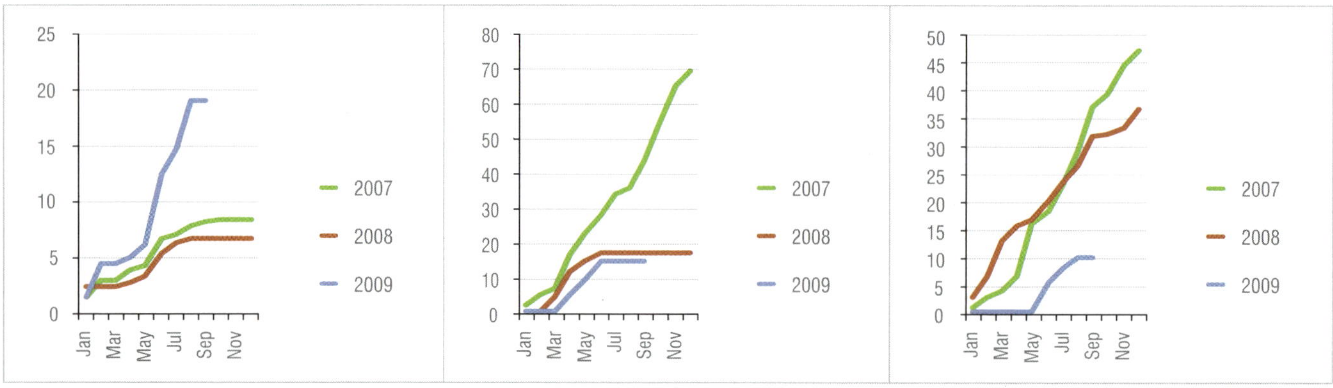

Sources: Dealogic and World Bank staff calculations.

years. Indonesia and the Philippines led with issuance of dollar-denominated government bonds of more than $2 billion each, half of which has been purchased by foreign investors. Nonresident purchases of local currency denominated debt have also rebounded throughout the region, mainly in Indonesia, Malaysia and Korea, because of improved investor confidence and expectations of currency appreciation (Figure 22). In Indonesia, nonresidents have purchased the equivalent of about $7 billion since March, offsetting net sales of similar size over the previous twelve months. Yields on ten-year rupiah denominated government bonds have fallen from about 14 percent in March to less than 10 percent at present, while the currency has strengthened 14 percent against the dollar, giving investors a return of more than 20 percent.

Equity investors have returned in force to some markets while reducing holdings in others. Equity inflows have risen strongly in Korea, where investors bought $19 billion worth of equities in the first half of the year and more thereafter, and in Indonesia with

Figure 22. Foreigners have resumed local bond purchases

(Nonresident holdings of local-currency government bonds, in trillions of Rupiah and billions of Ringgit)

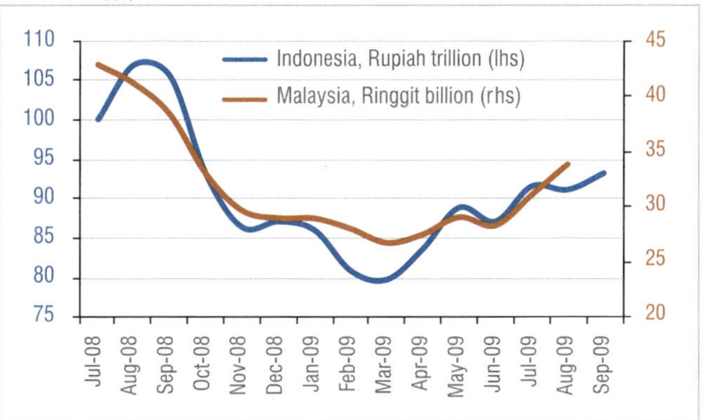

Source: Haver Analytics.

Figure 23. Equity prices in East Asia have risen faster than in developed countries this year

(Index, January 1, 2009=100)

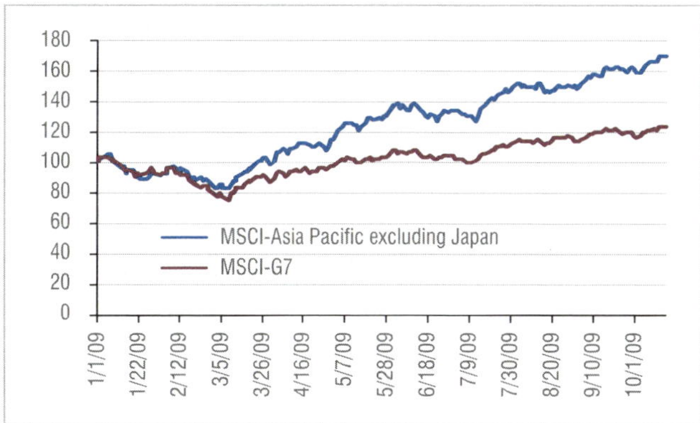

Sources: Datastream and Bloomberg.

$4 billion. These inflows compare with very large outflows from Hong Kong, China; Singapore; and Malaysia. It is likely that a substantial part of the $80 billion outflows from Hong Kong, China in the first half of 2009 and the whole of 2008 combined have been repatriated to China or invested in other countries in the region.

Investor optimism that the region's growth differential with the rest of the world will remain high, combined with renewed nonresident inflows have boosted equity prices strongly this year. Share prices gained 60 percent in East Asia on average from the start of 2009 through September, dwarfing the 20 percent rise on average in developed countries and broadly offsetting the decline during 2008 (Figure 23). The market for initial public offerings began to thaw by mid-2009 and was immediately overwhelmed by new or planned large IPOs, especially from China. In July, China State Construction Engineering Corporation, the country's largest homebuilder, raised the equivalent of $7.3 billion in the world's largest IPO in 16 months. The company received bids of $242 billion according to press reports, an amount equivalent to Malaysia's GDP. Although a stronger rebound in equity prices in East Asia is to be expected given perceptions about growth and the region's much increased role in the global economy, the speed of the increase has led to renewed concerns about speculative bubbles.

International financial conditions have improved but ongoing deleveraging among foreign banks is keeping cross-border flows depressed. Gross claims on developing East Asia fell by one-fourth, or about $140 billion, from the peak reached in mid-2008 to

Figure 24. Spreads on foreign bonds are back to pre-crisis levels

(In basis points over U.S. Treasuries, EMBIG)

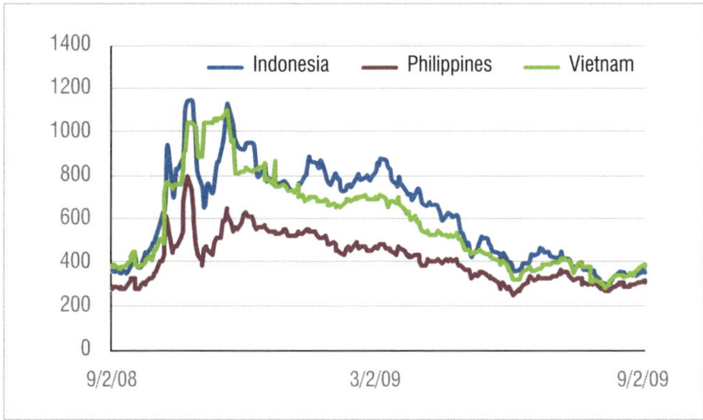

Source: JP Morgan.

Figure 25. Loans and other claims by foreign banks on East Asia have declined

(In billions of U.S. dollars, 1991-March 2009)

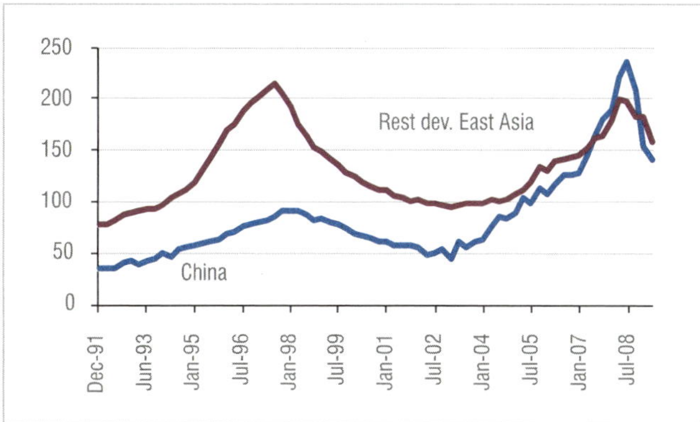

Source: BIS.

Box 1: China's Foreign Acquistions

	Outward FDI	o/w: acquisitions
	(In billions of U.S. dollars)	
2007	27	25
2008	56	20
2009	...	22
2000-2009	...	115

2009 Acquisitions

	Company	Sector	Country	Amount (In billions of US$)	Target
I. Successful aquistions				**21.9**	
Apr-09	CNPC, PetroChina	Oil/Gas	Kazakhstan	3.3	Kazmunajgaz
May-09	PetroChina	Oil	Singapore	1.0	Singapore Petroleum, 45.5 percent
May-09	Minmetals	Metals	Australia	0.9	OZ Minerals
Jun-09	Sinopec	Oil	Switzerland	7.2	Addax Petroleum
Jul-09	CNPC & Sinopec	Oil	Angola	1.3	Marathon Oils' field
Aug-09	Yanzhou Coal	Coal	Australia	2.9	Felix Resources
Sep-09	CIC	Oil/Gas	Kazakhstan	0.9	Kazmunajgaz
Oct-09	Jein Jein Nickel	Metals	Canada	2.0	Canadian Royalties
Oct-09	CIC	Oil	Russia	0.3	45 percent stake in Nobel Oil
Oct-09	PetroChina	Oil	Canada	2.0	Athabasca oil sands
II. Acquisitions in process					
Sep-09	Chinalco	Aluminum	Russia		A stake in UC Rusal, world's largest producer
Oct-09	CNOOC	Oil	Nigeria		Offshore oil fields
Oct-09	CNOOC	Oil	US		Norway Statoil's 20 of 451 drilling leases
III. Unsuccessful acquisitions					
Oct-09	China Nonferous Metals	Rare minerals	Australia		Australia requested stake in Lynas be cut below 50 percent
Sep-09	CNOOC	Oil	Nigeria	4.0	Kosmos stake in oil field
Jun-09	Chinalco	metals	Australia	19.5	Rio Tinto

Source: News agency reports. Prepared by Sepideh Khazai.

the end of the first quarter of 2009. In dollar terms, the decline has been the sharpest in China, reflecting a much steeper earlier surge that underscored concerns about bubbles fueled by foreign flows (Figure 25). Claims on Korea also fell sharply, reflecting concerns that lasted until early 2009 about large short-term foreign currency-denominated debt. Cross-border lending has begun increasing modestly as markets began to thaw around midyear, lifting this year's new loans to about $10 billion, or one-third of last year's level. Almost all syndicated loans to East Asia this year have been for short-term maturities, however, the renewed confidence in the region notwithstanding. This contrasts with 2007 when two-thirds of lending to Malaysia was long-term.

In contrast to the other categories of capital, net inflows of foreign direct investment (FDI) have fallen after the completion of earlier agreed deals boosted net inflows to a record high in the second half of 2008. Countries that are normally net FDI recipients (China, Indonesia, Malaysia, the Philippines and Thailand) reported lower inflows, and countries that are usually net

Figure 26. Corporate debt levels vary substantially across the region

(Debt in percent of assets)

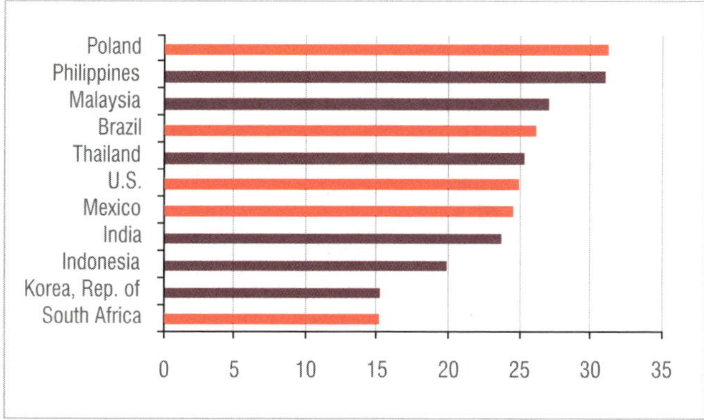

Sources: CEIC, Federal Reserve, IMF report 09/262.

Figure 27. Corporate profits are mostly down in 2009 */

(Percent change year-on-year)

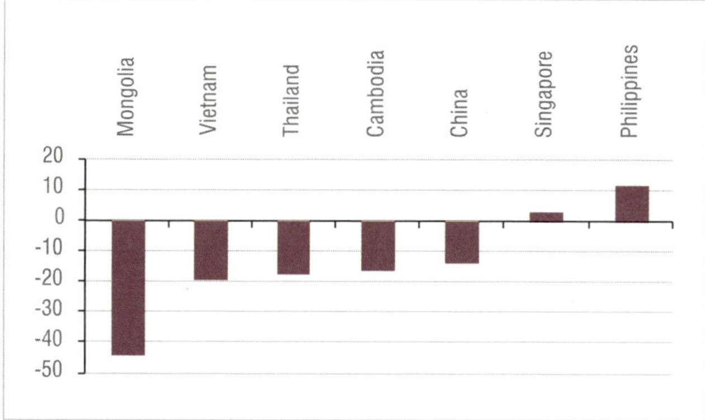

Sources: National authorities and World Bank staff calculations.
*/ Philippines: data for companies listed on the stock exchange (which represents a subset of all companies); China: industrial profits; all other countries: receipts of corporate income taxes in January-August, except for Cambodia where June to August is used, as the earlier period reflects payments of taxes on income from 2008.

FDI investors (Korea and Taiwan, China), reported reduced outflows. The Chinese authorities and public companies have used the crisis to increase investments abroad to earn higher returns on their large foreign exchange reserves (including the $200 billion of the country's foreign exchange reserves entrusted to the China Investment Corporation, CIC, the sovereign wealth fund) and, led by the large state-owned companies, secure access to much needed raw materials such as oil, coal and metals (Box 1: Acquisitions by Chinese entities abroad).

THE RISING TIDE IS NOT LIFTING ALL ENTERPRISES

The corporate sector is benefitting from the broad recovery, but with exports and production below pre-crisis levels, and financing conditions tighter for all but the large companies, many small enterprises remain under substantial stress. Measures to alleviate pressures on the small and medium enterprises (SMEs) have been adopted by several countries as part of fiscal stimulus packages, with the most comprehensive package in Korea where even before the crisis nearly half of all SMEs had interest burdens in excess of operating incomes. Efforts to support the small and micro enterprises, by contrast, have been limited.

The corporate sector entered the crisis in robust health in most countries after a decade of strong growth and efforts by governments and companies to reduce reliance on external borrowing and boost cash cushions. Leverage ratios were reduced substantially over the last decade, notably in the NIEs and the countries that suffered most in that crisis. Debt levels appeared reasonable even if somewhat higher for some countries given the policy bias in favor of capital-intensive development (Figure 26). Profitability was on a modest upward trend for years before the crisis, averaging about 8 percent for East Asia by 2008 as measured by return on assets.

The impact of the crisis on companies has varied across countries, sectors and corporate characteristics.

- Corporate profits fell substantially in most countries in the region in 2009 (Figure 27).[5] Indonesia, the Philippines and Lao PDR seem to be the main exceptions with rising profits. In Indonesia, the overall resilience of diverse enterprises serving

5 For China and the Philippines, corporate income tax receipts give similar information to data on corporate profits. Such data is not available for the other countries. Data are adjusted in countries where companies pay taxes in the current year on the basis of assessments for the previous year. For Cambodia, receipts from corporate income taxes account for less than 2 percent of GDP and may not be representative of the corporate sector, as the garment manufacturers - the companies hit worst by the recession - are still exempt from paying tax.

Figure 28. Profit growth in China has rebounded, levels still down for 2009

(In percent, year-on-year from 3-mo moving average)

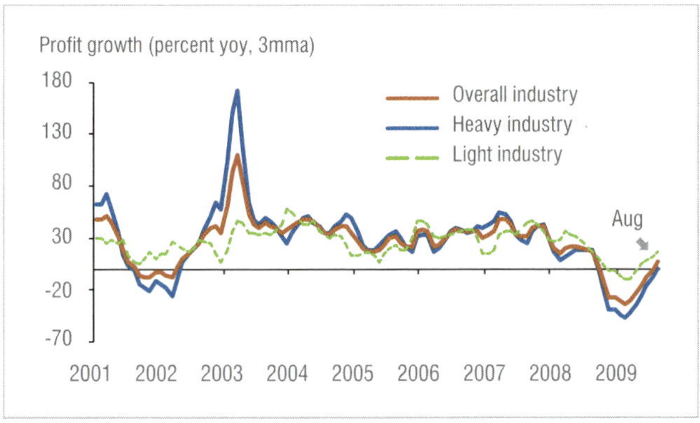

Source: Eric Le Borgne, S. Namingit and F. Loyola, 2009, Impact of the Global Crisis on the Philippines' Non-Financial Corporate Sector, the World Bank.

the large domestic economy has partly offset the negative impact of lower prices for commodity exports to limit the slowdown in profits to 8 percent in 2009 from 29 percent the previous year. In the Philippines, profits of the companies listed on the stock exchange are on track to rise 12 percent on average in 2009 after a 27 percent reduction in 2008. Since the listed companies in the Philippines include almost exclusively firms focused on the domestic market (such as real estate developers, retailers and banks) while companies in the electronics industry and most large exporters are not listed, the results reflect primarily the robust health of the domestic economy supported by much stronger than expected remittance inflows. Anecdotal evidence also suggests that companies in Lao PDR, all of them state-owned, have done well as they have continued to benefit from ongoing work on large energy projects financed from foreign investors, and construction of infrastructure facilities in preparation for the 25th Southeast Asian Games in December 2009.

- Corporate profit growth in China has rebounded strongly among most manufacturing, construction and utility companies. This was due to the infrastructure-focused stimulus package that included a surge in new bank lending, much of it directed to state enterprises. (Figure 28).

- The downturn hit export-oriented companies and small- and micro-enterprises the hardest. Companies that were part of global production networks faced a precipitous drop in orders and output in late 2008 and early 2009, prompting them to freeze investment and reduce labor costs. With balance sheets strong, most electronics companies preferred to retain staff, in part because of concerns that once a recovery starts they will have difficulty finding skilled workers (Box 2: Impact of the crisis on the electronics and electrical sector in Malaysia). In Cambodia, nearly a fifth of garment factories closed (many without paying final wages) and many more trimmed production substantially after the sharp decline in garment exports to the U.S., Cambodia's main market. Industries with a larger share of contract workers suffered a deeper cut in employment. Output and exports in the Thai automotive industry fell about 40 percent year-on-year in the first quarter of 2009, reducing capacity utilization in half and prompting companies to lay off or furlough about a third of the labor force, or 100,000 workers (equivalent to a third of the total job losses in the formal sector in Thailand).

- Most large retailers have weathered the crisis well, while informal retail outlets are experiencing sharply reduced sales in most countries. In the Philippines, a recently completed survey reveals that sales of informal garments, bags, shoes and electronics are down 35-40 percent in January-August from a year earlier, and a quarter of all owners of such outlets feel the crisis has not bottomed out yet.[6] Individuals in the minimum wage segment who have experienced the brunt of the crisis are now cautious to spend.

- The Business Process Outsourcing (BPO) industry in the Philippines remains a bright spot. Revenues are on track to increase 20 percent in 2009, despite a modest slowdown in the first half when the volume of voice services slowed because of difficulties among the main retail clients in the U.S. As the global recession intensified, so did the need for companies in developed

6 The survey was carried out by a team led by Eric le Borgne from the World Bank office in the Philippines during August 15 to September 15, 2009.

Box 2. Malaysia: Crisis, Recovery and Supply Chain Management, Insights from Japanese Multinationals in the Electrical and Electronics Sector[1]

The electrical and electronics (E&E) sector makes a large contribution to the economy of Malaysia, accounting for 38 percent of exports and 9 percent of GDP. The slump in foreign demand led to sharp production cuts among E&E companies and was a key contributor to the contraction in real GDP in the fourth quarter of 2008 and the first quarter of 2009 (Figure 1). With signs of recovery emerging, the industry is playing a similarly important part in the pickup of overall activity. Because of the significance of the E&E sector, it is essential to understand the impact of the crisis and the rebound at the firm level. What has allowed firms to cut production so quickly? How are firms seeing the prospects for the recovery?

Figure 1. The E&E Sector accounted for 55 percent of the GDP contraction in H1-2009

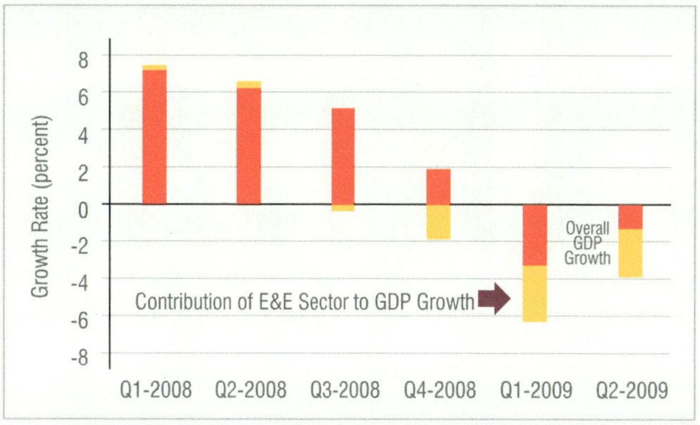

Focusing on the Japanese multinationals in the E&E sector, a subset of all manufacturers in Malaysia, we argue that a crucial role is played by the supply chain management practices of these firms.[2] Following decades of foreign direct investment, Japanese multinationals have contributed to the massive expansion of trade both between Malaysia and the rest of the region, and within Malaysia, as supporting industries have followed their larger clients. As a result of these developments, and thanks to the move towards less vertical integration of production within firms, there are now more than 1,300 Japanese and Japanese-related companies in Malaysia, and their supply chains embody complex linkages—both regionally and locally. As argued below, the efforts by firms to manage total supply chain costs provide important clues to the impact of the crisis and prospects for a recovery.

One of the most distinctive features of the recent crisis was the very rapid adjustment of production in response to cuts in forecasts for final demand. Purchase contracts for firms' output are usually specified on a monthly basis (depending on the level of customization of products). Therefore, when forecasts of final demand were reduced around September and October, buyers were able to cut their orders immediately, affecting deliveries starting in November and December. As orders for their products were cut, firms reduced or shut down production with minimal lag. This was thanks to the use of short-term supply contracts that matched contracts for their outputs, flexibility in adjusting labor costs, and improved management of inventories of both inputs and outputs (including the increased use of suppliers located in Malaysia). As a result, some of the companies interviewed cut production by 60-75 percent in December 2008.

Firms began cutting labor inputs by reducing hours, including second and third shifts, laying off contract laborers, and freezing hiring. Wage cuts were not reported, but companies shut down plants (especially around holidays) with proportional cuts in salary payments. Few regular staff were laid off, reflecting company concerns that they will not be able to hire workers with the same sets of skills given widely perceived shortages of skilled and semi-skilled labor. However, the contracts of many contract workers were not renewed. This was especially true of foreign workers who comprise as much as 40 percent of the labor force in the companies interviewed. Termination of contract workers appears to have been the main mechanism through which companies reduced headcount, with one firm reporting that its staff was reduced by 25 percent, mostly from cutting foreign contract workers. Other firms implemented hiring freezes, which reduced headcounts given normal attrition following the payment of year-end bonuses (staff turnover was reported to be very high in general, likely due to chronic labor shortages). Figure 2 illustrates how an actual firm accomplished labor reductions through turnover.

1 This box draws upon forthcoming study on Japanese supply chains in the E&E industry in Malaysia and Thailand, produced by Ratchada Anantavrasilpa, Kirida Bhaopichitr, Frederico Gil Sander, Rie Hikiji, and Philip Schellekens.

2 Companies interviewed included producers of semi-conductors, consumer electronics, electrical equipment and white goods, as well as suppliers to these companies.

Figure 2. This firm froze hiring in Q1-2009, resulting in a 20-percent cut in headcount from Q1-2008

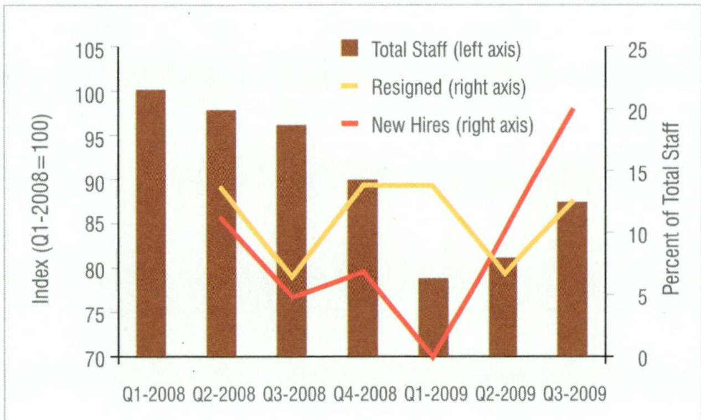

Adjustments to material inputs were linked to tight management of inventories, especially through the use of short-term supply contracts, information technology, and local suppliers. Supply contracts (including for business services, such as logistics), are usually adjusted quarterly and typically only specify prices and quality, while quantities are adjusted more frequently. Figure 3 shows an example for an actual firm that illustrates this point. In addition, a gradual move to local supporting industries also reduced the need for inventories. For example, a supplier who ten years ago had to buy critical inputs in bulk because of freight costs now can place orders from a local supplier on an almost daily basis. Finally, the use of information technology in supply chain management has allowed firms to have an accurate and timely picture of their input needs, inventory situation and orders, contributing to a quick transmission of final demand drop through the entire supply chain.

Some of the factors that contributed to the speed of the contraction are playing a role in the recovery. Because final demand dropped by less than forecast at the onset of the crisis, orders had to be filled from existing inventories. The advances in inventory management described earlier implied that inventory levels were low, so the drawdowns in inventories in the first quarter quickly led to new orders. The companies' ability to quickly adjust costs downward in the downturn protected their balance sheets, which were relatively healthy at the onset of the crisis anyway. The soundness of corporate balance sheets contributed to a quick restart of production, as few firms faced constraints to finance the working capital required. One additional reason for the financial soundness of a number of smaller Malaysian E&E firms has been lack of investment in recent years, which meant firms had higher levels of retained earnings that could be used as a buffer in case of a shock.

Figure 3. Inventories of this firm were cut (or increased) with about a one-month lag to change in sales

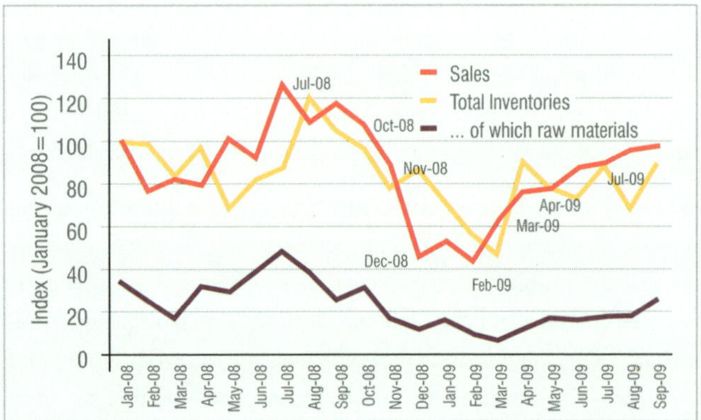

In other cases, responses to the crisis created frictions that slowed recovery, especially with respect to labor inputs, and shortage of semi-skilled and unskilled workers was widely reported in firm interviews. By April and May firms were already trying to re-hire workers, but they faced shortages. Firms attributed shortages partly to government efforts to reduce the economy's dependence on foreign workers, which contributed to delays in renewed labor inflows. Some companies claimed that production was still below order levels due to worker shortages and as a consequence were offering higher wages. Frictions created by suppliers' ability to restart production were also reported, but appeared less salient than labor issues.

Firms were unsure about the outlook for the recovery, but the impact of expectations within the supply chain is limited since in the near term firms are "expectations takers" from the parent companies. Improvements in inventory management have decreased the horizon of forecasting at the level of the firms within the supply chain, which are able to quickly ramp up production in response to increased orders – at least while capacity utilization is still well below potential. However, the uncertain outlook may have important implications in the medium-term, as some firms may delay capital expenditures needed to increase capacity. Because of limited vertical integration, bottlenecks may emerge that could initially limit the speed of the recovery.

Figure 29. Korea: overtime, temporary and part-time hours cut

(Average hours worked per month)

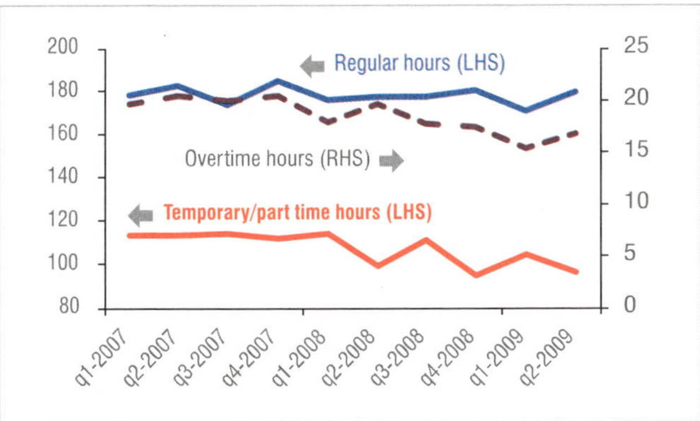

Sources: CEIC database and country statistical offices.
*/ For Thailand and Malaysia pre- crisis period is October 2007- April 2008 and post -crisis period is October 2008- April 2009. For the Philippines: October 2007- July 2008 vs. October 2008- July 2009. For Malaysia: October 2007- April 2008 vs. October 2008- April 2009. For Indonesia and Singapore: February-June 2008 and February-June 2009.

Figure 30. Out of manufacturing and into public services or retail trade

(In millions, second quarter of 2009 or latest available compared with a year earlier)

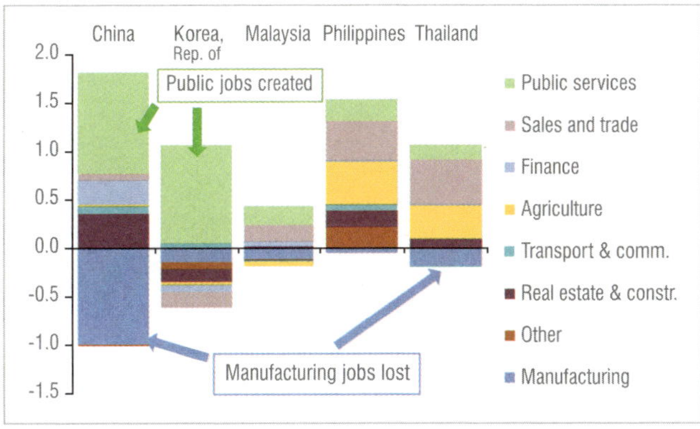

Sources: CEIC for China, Korea, and the Philippines; Labor Market Reports of the Department of Statistics for Malaysia; and the Thailand National Statistical Office.

economies to review their cost structures, operating processes, and value added chains. This is leading to a renewed wave of outsourcing with sectors that experienced large disruptions (e.g., banking) being the quickest to react: many large banking groups, as a result, are significantly expanding their presence in the Philippines. The global BPO sector is strategically looking for a back-up to India ("India plus one" strategy) and the Philippines seems to have established itself as the preferred choice given comparable costs, knowledge of English, and technical skills.

Government policies to support micro, small and medium-sized enterprises (MSMEs) have helped in some countries, but significant vulnerabilities remain especially for small and micro enterprises. In Thailand, MSMEs account for 99.7 percent of all registered firms, 38 percent of overall GDP and 76 percent of jobs created in a typical year before the crisis. While they continued to generate jobs during the downturn, absorbing the laid off formal sector workers in many cases, their incomes are reported to have declined by 20-40 percent on average. Tighter bank credit conditions, including the reduced availability of trade financing and the slowdown in remittances (that tend to finance investment for the small- and micro-enterprises), also disproportionally affected such firms.

THE CRISIS HAS AFFECTED WORKERS ACROSS SECTORS AND REGIONS

Enterprises – both formal and informal – adjusted to weaker demand through reducing hours worked and often through cutting wages and incomes and less often through letting workers go. Where workers were laid off in the formal sector, employers began by cutting temporary and part-time workers and only as a last resort did they reduce permanent employees. In Vietnam, as in many other countries in the region, factories have preferred to reduce the working hours of trained and skilled workers so as to contain eventual re-recruitment and training costs. In Korea, companies cut overtime, extra shifts and part-time workers, while preserving full-time workers that are backed by strict labor laws (Figure 29). In Thailand, the automotive sector cut a third of its labor force at the start of 2009, or 100,000 workers, and almost all of them were part-time or contract employees. In Cambodia, the number of working days of construction workers fell to 10-20 days a month for several months, while some garment workers work as few as 10 days.

Job losses were substantial in key export manufacturing sectors in many countries, but companies have begun hiring again since mid-2009. In China, Philippines and Thailand, employment in the manufacturing sector fell 2 percent year-on-year by April 2009,

Figure 31. Increases in unemployment rates have been limited */

(In percent, average for the year before September 2008 and the year after)

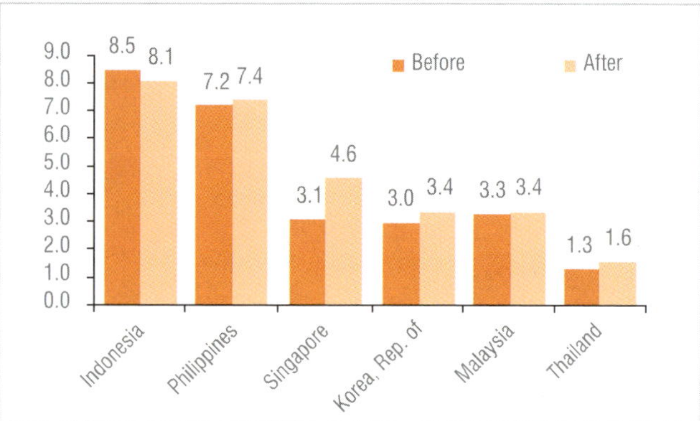

Sources: CEIC database and country statistical offices.
*/ For Thailand and Malaysia pre- crisis period is October 2007- April 2008 and post -crisis period is October 2008- April 2009. For the Philippines: October 2007- July 2008 vs. October 2008- July 2009. For Malaysia: October 2007- April 2008 vs. October 2008- April 2009. For Indonesia and Singapore: February-June 2008 and February-June 2009.

Figure 32. Indonesia: employment dislocations are spatially concentrated

(Percent of provincial workforce vulnerable)

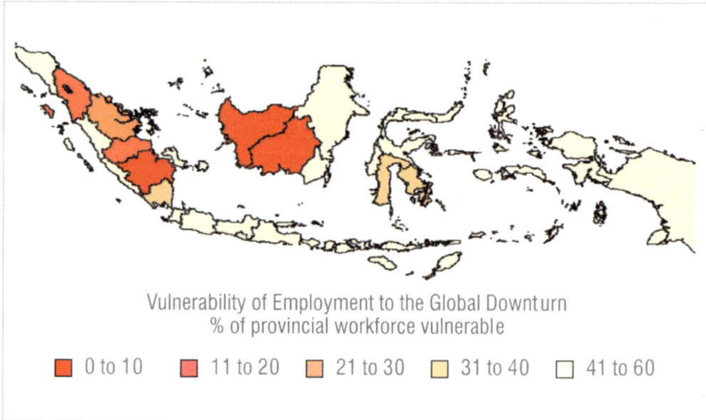

Sources: World Bank, (2009) Indonesia Quarterly, Weathering the Storm, June 2009.
Note: "Vulnerable employment" is defined as employment in crisis-affected sectors.

when job losses in manufacturing appear to have troughed. Factories in China's coastal regions now report shortages. In Thailand, automotive factories added a second shift to their production in August after eliminating it in January, and have begun hiring temporary and contract workers anew. In Malaysia, companies in a segment of the electronics sector (as described in Box 2) froze hiring in the first quarter of 2009 and refused to renew contracts of contract workers, resulting in a 20 percent reduction in headcount in the first quarter of 2009 from a year earlier. A few months later, however, companies have begun looking for new workers but are reporting shortages. In Cambodia, by contrast, there is scant evidence that companies are moving to boost employment after laying off 65,000 workers earlier this year.

Workers let go have typically found jobs either in other sectors or more often in the informal sector at lower pay. In China, Korea, and the Philippines, job losses in the manufacturing sector were accompanied by job creation in agriculture, trading, and construction, with large share of the jobs in some countries in the informal sector. Moreover in China, Korea and the Philippines, new publicly financed jobs were created as a result of the fiscal stimulus packages (Figure 30). As a result, unemployment rose by less than half a percentage point on average in the year after the crisis compared with the year before the crisis, except in Indonesia (where it fell) and in Singapore (Figure 31). Nonetheless, the significant proportion of job creation in agriculture and the wholesale and retail sectors during the crisis suggests that many workers have moved into marginal urban jobs as a coping strategy. Though specific data are scarce, qualitative assessments of the crisis suggest that this shift has increased competition among informal enterprises and put downward pressure on incomes.

The impact of the employment dislocations have typically been spatially concentrated., given the rising role of agglomeration economies in the region. In Indonesia, vulnerable jobs are spatially concentrated in the few regions that produce estate crops for which world prices have dropped significantly and where local economies are relatively undiversified, such as parts of Kalimantan and Sumatra (Figure 32).

The crisis has affected workers across genders and across the income distribution. In Cambodia, the three most affected sectors have been export manufacturing (garments), construction, and tourism. Layoffs in the garment sector have affected workers at all levels of income given the fairly even income distribution for such employees. In the construction sector, meanwhile, the bulk of the workers are poor, while a small share of employees are poor in the tourism industry. Although much attention has focused on the impacts of the crisis on female workers who are concentrated in the garment sector, the data suggest that male workers, concentrated in the construction sector, have also been quite vulnerable during the crisis.

Figure 33. Cambodia: the impact of the crisis is felt by both the poor and the non-poor ...

(Percent of total employed in sector)

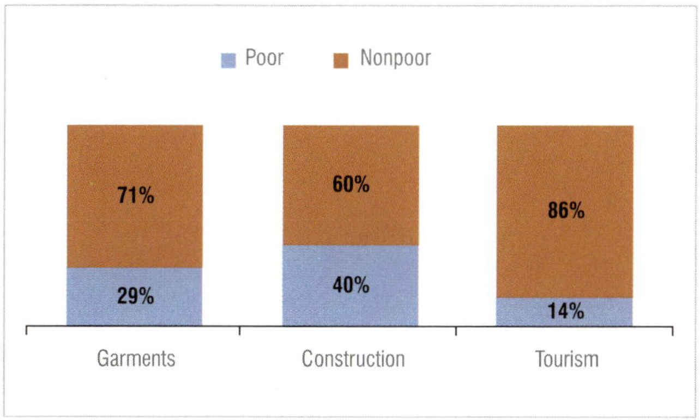

Source: Cambodia Statistics Office.

Figure 34. ... and across the gender divide

(Percent of total employed in sector)

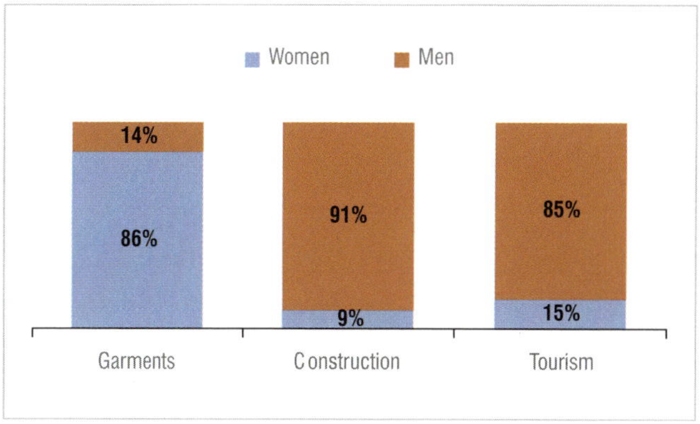

Source: Cambodia Statistics Office.

Figure 35. Due to the crisis, 14 million more people will be in poverty in 2010 */

(In millions)

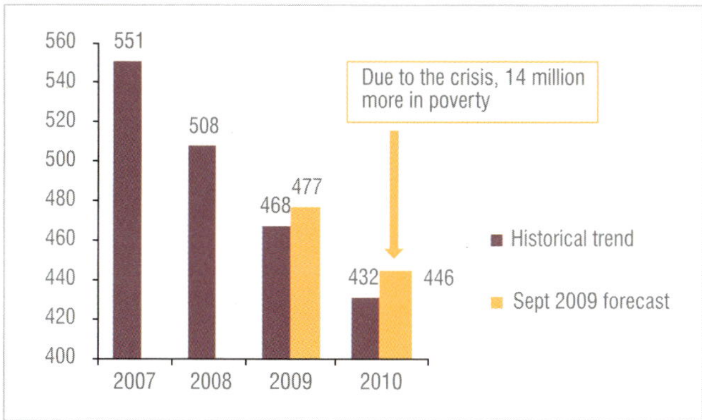

Source: World Bank staff estimates.
Note: Estimates using a poverty line of $2-a-day (purchasing power parity), calculated as the difference between: (a) the poverty headcount in 2010 that would have resulted had historical (2001-2005) growth rates persisted and (b) poverty headcount in 2010 using current growth projections in the form of the crisis.

Figure 36. Most of the additional poor will be in middle-income countries

(In millions)

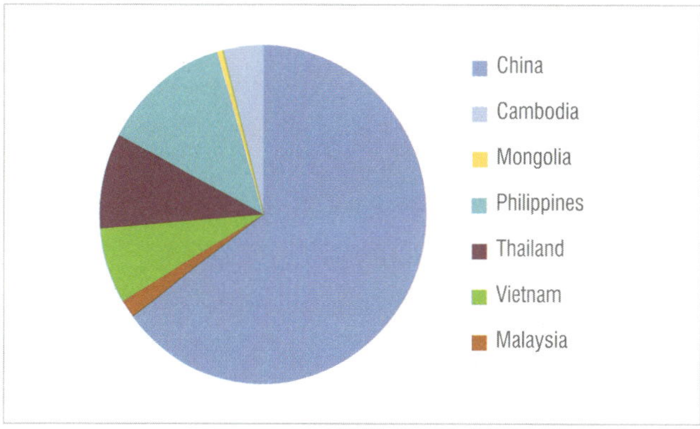

Source: World Bank staff estimates.
2010 using current growth projections in the form of the crisis.

THE PACE OF POVERTY REDUCTION HAS SLOWED

The crisis has slowed the pace of poverty reduction in the region. It is estimated that there will be about 9 million more extreme and moderate poor in the region – people earning less than $2 day – in 2009 and 14 million more extreme and moderate poor in the region in 2010 as a result of the crisis (Figure 35).[7] These numbers are about eight million lower than our projections from April 2009, primarily because of upward revisions of our growth projections. As in our earlier assessments, most of the additional poor will come from the large middle- income countries because of the sheer size of the population there. China is projected to account for nearly 9 million of the additional estimated poor (Figure 36). The additional estimated poor coming from the smaller, low income countries in the region is expected to be around 5 million. All of these projections are subject to substantial uncertainty, both because of risks to the global and regional economic outlook, but also given the lack of higher frequency data on

7 With rapid income growth and the emergence of several middle-income countries in the region since the 1990s, consideration of a poverty benchmark higher than the absolute poverty line of $1.25 a day is being increasingly dominant in policy discussions. The $2 a day poverty line has more relevance for poverty is used in this update to maintain greater policy relevance.

disaggregated household incomes and consumption. Even when such data are available, interpretation may be challenging, with additional complications for the appropriate policy response (see Box 3, Philippines: The Growth-Poverty Nexus).

Box 3. Philippines: The Growth-Poverty Nexus

Weak economic growth has been a long-standing problem in the Philippines, and largely accounted for the slow progress made in poverty reduction during the 1980s and 1990s. When economic growth finally accelerated after 2001, expectations were raised that poverty would henceforth fall at a faster pace. These hopes were dashed by the 2006 household survey, which indicated that the improved economic performance had not translated into poverty reduction. Rather than declining, the poverty headcount ratio was unchanged in 2006 compared with 2000, and actually increased relative to 2003.

Poverty Estimates based on Constant (2006) National Poverty Lines

	Poverty Headcount Ratios		
	2000	2003	2006
Urban	16.8	17.3	19.5
Rural	44.7	44.4	45.9
Total	**31.0**	**31.1**	**32.9**
	Official estimates based on variable poverty lines		
	33.0	**30.0**	**32.9**

Source: World Bank, based on FIES 2000-2003-2006

Why has poverty not declined since 2000? The stronger real GDP growth during 2000-2006 according to national account statistics (NA) is in contrast to data from the Philippines household surveys that indicate average real household income and consumption were steadily declining during this period. According to the Family Income and Expenditure Surveys (FIES), from which the poverty indicators are drawn, average per capita consumption declined by 1.5 percent a year. This removes all mystery from the observed increase in poverty after 2003, since it only confirms the commonly observed negative relationship between poverty and growth in consumption. Instead, what remains puzzling is that the NA data indicate annual per capita growth of more than 2 percent a year in 2000-06, while the FIES surveys show negative growth.

Per Capita Income and Expenditures in the Philippines

(In percent, average annual growth rates in constant prices)

	1985-1997	2000-03	2003-06	2000-06
	Based on data from household surveys			
Expenditures per capita	2.7	-0.9	-0.5	-0.7
Income per capita	na	-1.7	-1.2	-1.4
	Based on national accounts data			
Consumption per capita	1.7	2.3	3.5	2.9
GDP per capita	1.4	1.7	3.6	2.7

Sources: The household survey-based figures refer to the Family Income and Expenditure Survey; the figures up to 1997 are from the World Bank (2001), Philippines Poverty Assessment, and the figures as of 2000 are from the Philippines National Statistics Office. The National Accounts-based growth rates are from the World Bank Development Database.

It turns out that the divergence between survey- and NA-based growth data is not unique to the Philippines. As noted by Angus Deaton (2006) in a comprehensive cross-country review,[1] NA estimates are typically, though not always, larger than survey-based estimates, and there is a tendency for the National Accounts-based estimates to grow more rapidly than the survey-based estimates. He also notes that household survey data generally underestimate real consumption and income growth (mainly because the more affluent households are generally under-represented in the survey samples), while NA data tend to over-estimate growth (primarily on account of measurement conventions in the compilation of GDP).[2] Even though the National Accounts tend to over-estimate growth, however, an abundance of anecdotal evidence (e.g., export growth, corporate profits) indicates that, on balance, aggregate economic growth has been positive during 2000-06. Similarly, reports from the Philippines' Social Weather Station corroborate the finding that poverty has not declined. This suggests that the growth that did take place during that period in the Philippines must also have been associated with a deteriorating distribution of income. This is a matter of concern, as the country already exhibits among the highest degrees of income inequality in the region.

1 Deaton, Angus (2005), "Measuring Poverty in a Growing World (or Measuring Growth in a Poor World)" Review of Economics and Statistics, Vol. LXXXVIII, No. 1, February, page 6.

2 There may also be shortcomings in the quality of the Philippines National Accounts that have exacerbated the overestimation of GDP growth. See, Medalla, F. and K. Jandoc (2008), "Philippine GDP Growth after the Asian Financial Crisis: Resilient Economy or Weak Statistical System?", University of the Philippines, School of Economics Discussion Paper No. 0802, May.

II. ECONOMIC POLICIES SUPPORTING RECOVERY IN EAST ASIA

FISCAL POLICIES HAVE BEEN EASED SUBSTANTIALLY

Fiscal easing, including through implementation of fiscal stimulus measures, has helped support domestic demand in most countries in the region. As the crisis hit, the headlines were focused on the fiscal stimulus measures enacted by all of the region's middle-income countries and the NIEs. In our update issued in April ("Battling the Forces of Global Recession"), we estimated that the announced fiscal stimulus packages among these countries and Vietnam amounted to about 3.6 percent of regional GDP, with measures worth 1.7 percent of GDP to be implemented in 2009.[8] We now estimate that the fiscal stimulus in the region's middle-income countries would amount to 2.1 percent of GDP in 2009, as most countries increased spending by more than planned earlier either by announcing additional stimulus packages or accelerating expenditure plans already in the pipeline (Figure 37 and Table 2). Even if stimulus spending in some countries falls short of projections because of delays in disbursements on infrastructure projects, the outcome for the year as a whole will be almost as large as the stimulus estimated for the G-20 of about 2 percent, and will compare favorably with the outcome in the U.S. (2.4 percent), the eurozone (1.5 percent) and Japan (3.5 percent) (Figure 38). Automatic stabilizers, however, are also supporting domestic incomes and demand, although they are smaller in the region than in the advanced economies.

During the year, several of the low-income and resource-rich countries in the region implemented substantial spending increases that were considered less likely at the start of the year. The discretionary stimulus injected by the governments of Cambodia and Lao PDR, amounted to about 3 percent of GDP, larger than many of the region's middle-income countries. Contrary to earlier expectations that low-income countries would limit spending increases to additional foreign aid, the countries primarily financed additional spending by drawing down domestic deposits, borrowing from domestic banks and direct lending by the central bank (in Lao PDR). Among the resource-rich countries that were able to save substantial portion of earlier windfall gains from high commodity prices, PNG boosted spending by about 5 percent of non-oil GDP.

Figure 37. Most countries delivered more fiscal stimulus than announced

(in percent of GDP)

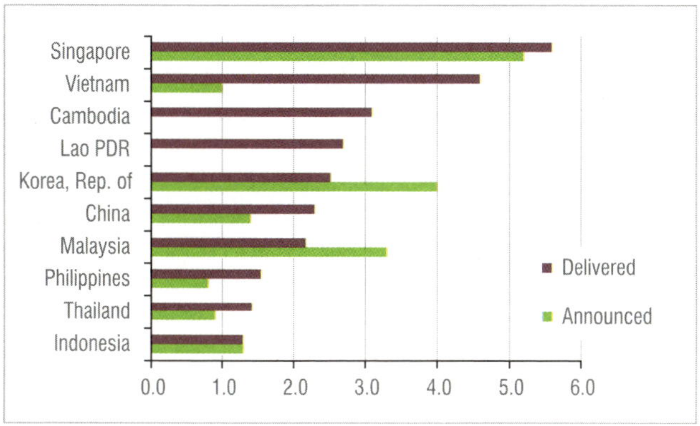

Sources: National authorities and staff estimates and projections.

Table 2. Fiscal deficits have risen due to fiscal stimulus packages and weaker economic activity

(in percent of GDP)

	2007	2008	2009
Cambodia	-2.9	-2.2	-6.7
China	0.6	-0.4	-3.3
Indonesia	-1.3	-0.1	-2.4
Korea, Rep. of	3.8	1.2	-2.5
Lao PDR	-2.8	-2.0	-6.7
Malaysia	-3.2	-4.8	-7.8
Mongolia	2.8	-5.0	-6.5
Philippines	-1.7	-1.5	-3.8
Singapore	7.3	12.4	4.2
Thailand	-1.7	-1.1	-4.2
Vietnam	-5.3	-4.2	-9.4

Sources: National authorities and Bank staff projections.

8 This calculation refers only to the fiscal stimulus to be implemented only by central governments, which in China is only a third of the RMB 4 trillion infrastructure-stimulus package; in Malaysia is about half of the MYR 67 billion total of the first and second stimulus packages, and in the Philippines is about two-thirds of the PHP 330 billion resiliency package. There are other elements in fiscal stimulus packages in the packages of the other countries in the region that do not immediately affect the central government budget. The headline number of all announced stimulus packages in the region's middle-income countries and the NIEs was equivalent to 9.4 percent of their GDP, with measures equivalent to 5 percent of GDP to be implemented in 2009.

Figure 38. Fiscal stimulus implemented in East Asia compares favorably with that in advanced countries

(in percent of GDP)

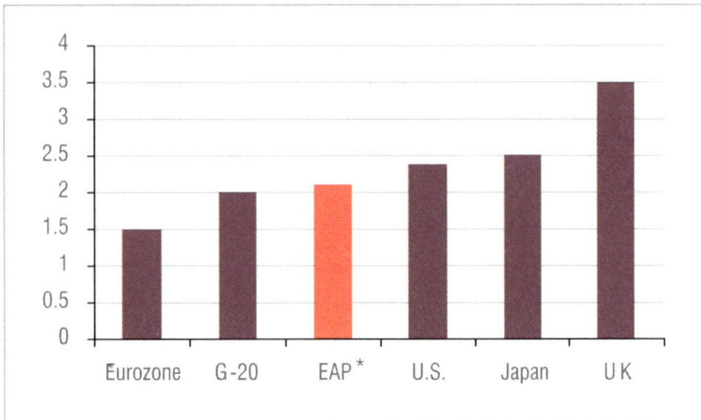

Sources: National authorities and staff estimates and projections. */EAP denotes East Asia and the Pacific.

Figure 39. Fiscal stimulus has been biased toward expenditures

(in percent of total stimulus)

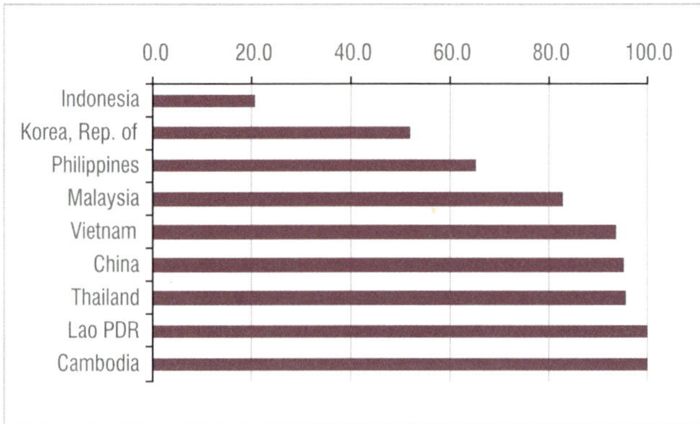

Sources: National authorities and Bank staff estimates.

Tax cuts, a category of stimulus that is the fastest to implement but is understood to have a lower short-term impact on economic activity, accounted for about one-sixth of the overall stimulus packages in the region in 2009. Only Indonesia and Korea relied on tax cuts for the bulk of their packages, emphasizing reductions in personal income taxes in the former and corporate income taxes in the latter (Figure 39).

Countries in the region increased support for the poor and vulnerable. Measures included targeted and untargeted social transfers (China, Indonesia, Korea, the Philippines and Thailand), vouchers to low-income or rural households (in some cities in China, Indonesia, and Taiwan, China), school feeding and other such schemes, and support for housing (in addition to the construction of low-income housing in China, Indonesia and Thailand). Although such support has been crucial for limiting hardship, the support in most cases was not well targeted given the lack of properly developed social protection systems in the region.

The impact of fiscal stimulus packages has varied from strongly positive in China, Singapore and Korea, to limited in Indonesia, Malaysia and Thailand. In general, the limits to countercyclical fiscal policy in countries with open economies, notably Malaysia and Thailand, are well known. Stimulus that was dominated by infrastructure and targeted social spending appears to have had the largest impact, while those focused on tax cuts and untargeted social transfers and wage increases have been least effective. In China, the government forcefully front-loaded the overall RMB4 trillion infrastructure stimulus package and combined it with a surge in bank lending to help activity bottom out in the first quarter of 2009. In Singapore and Korea, the fiscal stimulus also caused activity to rebound strongly, as it was focused on schemes to generate new jobs, support bank lending and SMEs, and accelerate already planned infrastructure spending. The inclusion of untargeted social transfers in fiscal stimulus packages, such as in Malaysia and Thailand, also led to a somewhat more limited impact on activity. Long implementation lags in Malaysia, moreover, mean that the impact on domestic demand will be felt more in late 2009 and in 2010. The fiscal package in Indonesia dominated by tax cuts did little to support economic activity; rather, it was pre-election spending that provided a more important and timely boost.

Some countries, notably China, are using their fiscal stimulus packages to advance medium-term goals. An important aspect of China's stimulus package is the extent of its investment in energy efficiency and low-carbon alternatives to road and air transport. The government is spending the equivalent of $90 billion on new rail projects in 2009, with a similar amount planned for next year. China will also spend an average $31 billion per year on energy conservation, pollution reduction and ecological improvement in 2009-11 and another $54 billion on technological upgrades in industrial restructuring in energy intensive sectors.

Figure 40. Credit growth has accelerated this year in China and Vietnam ...

(percent change year-on-year)

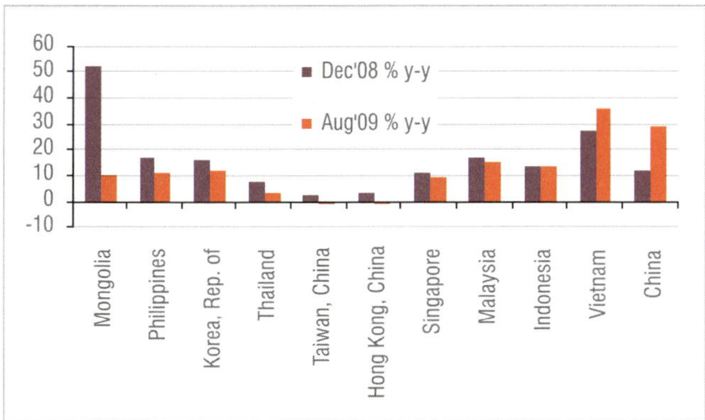

Source: CEIC.

Figure 41. ... boosting substantially the level of credit to GDP

(in percent of GDP)

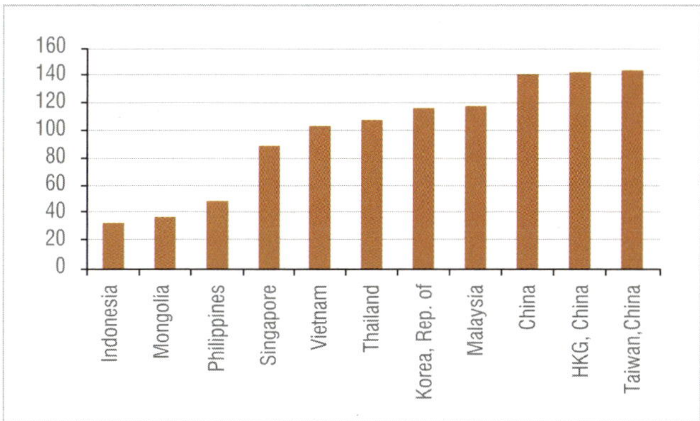

Source: CEIC.

Figure 42. Housing prices have rebounded sharply ...

(in percent since January 2009) */

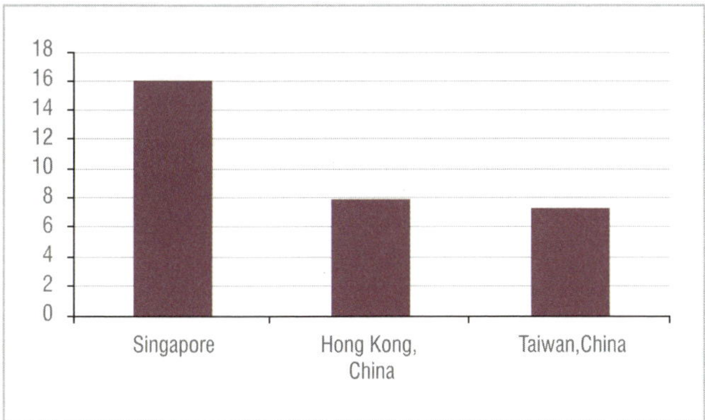

Source: CEIC. */In Singapore, during the third quarter of 2009.

Figure 43. ... as have property sales in China

(residential floor space, % change year-on-year)

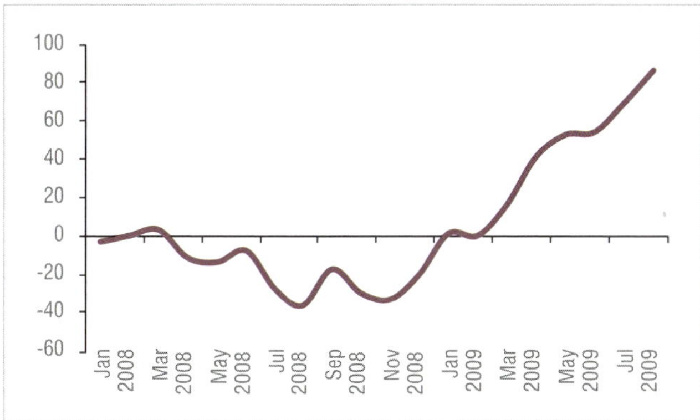

Source: CEIC.

MONETARY EASING HAS SUPPORTED THE RECOVERY

With price pressures subdued, the monetary authorities in the region have maintained monetary accommodation, including low policy rates, reduced reserve requirements and other exceptional measures to support economic activity and facilitate financial institutions' access to ample liquidity. Loose monetary policy in China resulted in a surge in bank lending that provided local governments and state-owned companies with the complementary resources needed to carry out the infrastructure-focused stimulus program. As a result, new bank credit extended in China in 2009 amounted to the equivalent of one-third of GDP, raising the ratio of credit to GDP to 141 percent, the highest in the region together with Hong Kong, China and Taiwan, China. Credit growth has also accelerated in Vietnam since the start of the year, leading to concerns that credit may be fueling asset price bubbles in both countries (Figure 40 and Figure 41).

Concerns about asset price bubbles are reinforced by the rapid increase in equity and housing prices across the region. Sales of real estate have also risen strongly, notably in China; Hong Kong, China; and Singapore (Figure 42 and Figure 43). In Singapore, the 16 percent surge in property prices during the third quarter led the authorities to ease capacity constraints by releasing more land for development and to take steps not to allow borrowers to defer payments. Some central banks could set targets for the overall rate of growth of bank credit, establish caps on the share of bank lending for real estate and portfolio investments, and ban loans for short-selling – similar to what Vietnamese did in early 2008. Other measures that supervisors could use include higher collateral requirements, higher capital requirements for riskier lenders and mandatory lower loan-to-value and loan-to-repayment ratios for mortgage lending – as the monetary authority in Hong Kong, China did recently for larger mortgages.

EXCHANGE MARKET INTERVENTION LIMITED CURRENCY APPRECIATION

China's de-facto peg to a weakening US dollar has forced the authorities in most East Asian countries to intervene heavily in foreign exchange markets to limit appreciation of their own currencies (Figure 44). The view that stronger exchange rates will be important in extracting more growth from domestic demand is yet to take firmer hold. Moreover, central banks in the region continue to show little tolerance for exchange rate volatility, even if countries such as Indonesia, Korea and Vietnam adjusted well to the adverse demand shock by allowing their currencies to weaken last year, thus limiting the drawdown on reserves. Going forward, exchange rate flexibility will be critical in managing foreign exchange inflows while keeping inflation and asset price increases in check.

Figure 44. Limited appreciation after the crisis

(percent change in nominal effective exchange rates)

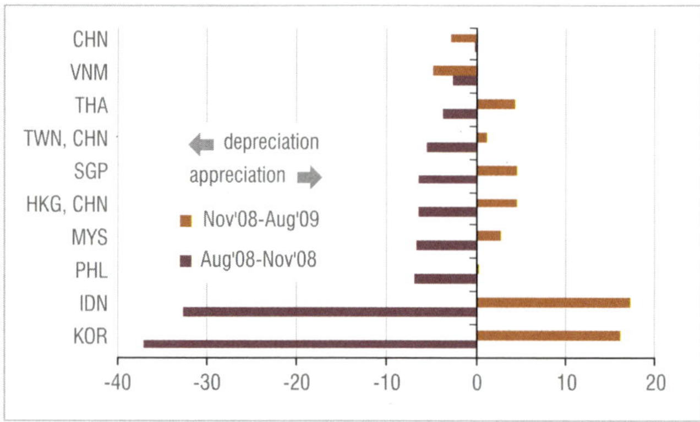

Source: IMF INS.

SOCIAL POLICY HAS HELPED AMELIORATE THE IMPACT OF THE CRISIS ON THE POOR[9]

East Asian country governments, especially in the large middle income countries, have implemented several measures to cushion the impact of the slowdown on the most vulnerable. Policy responses have been helped by the smaller than expected negative impact of the crisis on unemployment and labor incomes. At the same time, the effectiveness of the responses has been limited by the lack of adequately structured and financed social safety nets in most countries.

As the economic crisis came on the heels of the food and fuel crisis that hit the region in 2008, all of the middle-income countries and Vietnam had already introduced social protection measures before the economic downturn accelerated at the turn of 2009. In the Philippines, the government scaled up the existing conditional cash transfer program (Pantawid Pamilyang Pilipino Program or 4P) by increasing its budget tenfold and Indonesia reinstated targeted unconditional transfer (Bantuan Langsung Tunai –BLT) it had first used in 2005 in response to high fuel prices. In China, rural health insurance was expanded and deepened and allocation to earthquake reconstruction in Sichuan Province was increased considerably. Even in the low-income countries including Cambodia and Laos, actions to address the food and fuel crisis provided a stepping stone to build a more systematic response to the economic downturn, and partnerships continued with donors and NGOs on cash- and food-for-work programs that were particularly well suited to countries with lower capacity.

9 This section draws heavily from: ASEAN and World Bank (2009) "ASEAN Assessment on the Social Impacts of the Global Financial Crisis: A Snap-shot Report for notation at the 15th ASEAN Summit, Thailand, 23 October 2009"

Additional social protection measures implemented during the crisis have depended on available fiscal space and institutional capacity. Cash transfers, both targeted and untargeted, were combined with in-kind transfers in Vietnam and all middle-income countries except Indonesia, extended benefits under existing social safety nets (Cambodia, China and the Philippines), and subsidies to households for health and education (the Philippines and Thailand).

The investments in infrastructure supported under the fiscal stimulus packages have also had a substantial positive labor impact. China's infrastructure-focused stimulus package has captured the headlines. But the stimulus packages in Indonesia, Philippines, Vietnam, and Thailand also included community-based small-scale infrastructure projects that were designed to create temporary employment opportunities.[10]

Subsidies for worker training were also a common element in the region's stimulus packages. Malaysia has provided employers with monetary incentives to retain or hire employees and provide training, and Thailand devoted significant stimulus funds to subsidized capacity building programs. Special skills training program have also been implemented in China, Cambodia and Laos.

The crisis has underscored the urgency of developing a more coherent approach to social protection in the region, including through selective social insurance schemes. In the Philippines, additional benefits have been provided to members of various social security institutions, while in China significant efforts were made to increase pension benefits, expand rural pension schemes, and broaden rural health insurance. The latter measures have been implemented in addition to increasing the threshold for minimum living allowance under China' Dibao program and providing a one- time income support for 74 million poor.

10 Thailand's Sufficiency Economy Community Project, Indonesia's Community Empowerment Program, Vietnam's program for the 61 poorest districts, and the Comprehensive Livelihood and Emergency Employment Program in the Philippines are all examples of community-based approaches to mitigating the social impacts of the crisis.

III. TRANSFORMING THE REBOUND INTO RECOVERY

The economies of East Asia and the Pacific have rebounded sharply from the steep drop in activity in early 2009, thanks to fiscal and monetary stimulus, substantially improved global financial conditions, and an upturn in the inventory cycles. We are revising our projection for regional growth for 2009 up by 1.3 percentage points compared to our April forecast ("Battling the Forces of Global Recession" issued on April 6, 2009) even as our forecast for developed economies in 2009 are further downgraded. Real GDP in the G-3 is now projected to fall 3.5 percent in 2009 compared with a projected decline of only 0.4 percent a year ago and 3.1 percent in April, while projections of global trade volumes are now revised to show a contraction of 11.4 percent versus a drop of 2.1 percent forecast a year ago (Table 3).

Growth in the developed economies is projected to recover at a modest pace in 2010, as banks continue to deleverage, and high and rising unemployment subdues the recovery in private consumption. Global capital flows are likely to recover moderately from the lows of 2009 but will remain smaller than the record highs reached in 2007 as cross-border lending continues to suffer from international banks recognizing credit losses (now about half of the total projected) while inflows of foreign direct investment remain limited by large excess capacity.

Table 3. Growth projections are revised up
(Percent change y-y unless indicated otherwise)

				Prev Forecasts Dec'08	Prev Forecasts Apr'09
	2008	2009f	2010f	2009	2009
Developing East Asia	8.0	6.7	7.8	6.7	5.3
China	9.0	8.4	8.7	7.5	6.5
Indonesia	6.1	4.3	5.4	4.4	3.4
Malaysia	4.6	-2.3	4.1	3.7	-1.0
Philippines	3.8	1.4	3.1	3.0	1.9
Thailand	2.6	-2.7	3.5	3.6	-2.7
Vietnam	6.2	5.5	6.5	6.5	5.5
Cambodia	6.7	-2.2	4.2	4.9	-1.0
Lao PDR	7.3	6.4	7.5	6.0	5.0
Timor-Leste	12.8	7.4	8.0	1.4	1.0
Mongolia	8.9	0.5	3.0	7.5	2.7
Fiji	0.2	-0.3	1.8	1.1	2.4
Papua New Guinea	6.6	3.9	3.7	5.0	4.7
Memoranda:					
Developing East Asia					
Middle-income countries	8.1	6.9	7.9	6.8	5.4
Low-income countries	6.3	4.5	6.0	6.1	4.7
Excluding China					
Developing East Asia	4.7	1.1	4.5	4.1	1.1
Middle-income countries	4.5	0.7	4.3	3.8	0.7
G-3	0.3	-3.5	2.0	-0.4	-3.1
Global trade volumes	3.2	-11.4	4.0	-2.1	-6.0

Sources: Datastream; DECPG; and World Bank staff estimates and projections. f=forecast

East Asia may receive a larger share of these inflows because of a combination of investor expectations of stronger growth in the region than the rest of the world, the potential for currency appreciation and the growing liquidity and sophistication of the region's financial markets. Although limited availability of capital is a key risk, a surge in capital flows will create a separate set of challenges.

Premature withdrawal of fiscal and monetary stimulus is among the key concerns of policymakers in the region, just as it was on top of the agenda during the recent meeting of the G20 heads of state in Pittsburgh. Nonetheless, as growth recovers broadly and inflation pressures begin to materialize, monetary policy may need to be tightened sooner rather than later in East Asia, following the recent policy rate hikes by the central banks in Israel, Australia, and Norway. It is more likely that the monetary authorities in East Asia will move first by removing some of the support for liquidity in domestic and foreign currencies (similar to the reabsorption of foreign currency liquidity by the Korean authorities which they had extended to the market earlier), returning reserve requirements to pre-crisis levels (following up on the steps of Indonesia's central bank) and scaling back the scope for collateral eligible for accessing central bank facilities before hiking policy rates.

Governments in the region plan to continue implementing already announced fiscal stimulus packages until the recovery is on firmer footing. Moreover, some governments have announced additional stimulus measures, including in Thailand and Singapore. The Thai government is boosting spending with a second stimulus package equivalent to 16 percent of GDP to be spent over 2010-2012 to largely alleviate critical transportation bottlenecks. About a third of the package will be within the central government budget, and the rest off-budget. In Singapore, the government decided to extend for six months the Jobs Credit Scheme, a key and successful part of its stimulus program that was set to expire this year. Balancing between projections for ongoing recovery and concerns that activity may weaken again, the government is reducing the amount of subsidy under the program that encourages new hiring, but is keeping it operational to allow for more rapid response in case of economic weakness. Other governments have drafted budgets that allow for discretionary increases should economic activity weaken. This is the case in Indonesia, where the government targets the 2010 deficit to narrow to 1.6 percent of GDP from 2.2 percent in 2008, but the budget authorizes the government to enact new spending and boost the deficit to 2 percent of GDP should the recovery of growth sputter.

The low-income countries will remain under pressure to support domestic demand. Some, including Lao PDR, are planning to sustain large fiscal deficits to be financed from government deposits and the domestic banks. Other countries, such as Mongolia, are set to carry out somewhat tighter fiscal policy under the IMF-supported program. The continued need to mobilize resources from the multilateral institutions to help the most vulnerable remains a priority, as emphasized by the recent Leaders' G-20 summit held in Pittsburgh.

The authorities in the region are aware that the limits of what fiscal policy could accomplish in stimulating domestic demand will be reached faster unless investors are reassured that exit strategies will be put in place to unwind the stimulus when recovery sets in more firmly. Such strategies will be more credible if supported by robust medium-term fiscal and debt frameworks. Coordinated withdrawal of stimulus, much like the coordinated introduction of the extraordinary fiscal support will be important, as emphasized at the recent leaders' summit of the G20.

Helped by large and timely fiscal and monetary support and on the basis of strong fundamentals before the crisis, growth in developing East Asia is projected to reach 6.7 percent in 2009, the same pace of expansion we forecast a year ago. But the composition of growth is expected to be fundamentally different from what we projected a year ago, however. On the expenditure side, the contribution of net exports turned substantially more negative in China after several years of increasingly stronger boost to output, and the contribution of private investment is also negative in almost all countries. Government spending, by contrast, whether on consumption or investment, has contributed more than expected earlier as stimulus spending was either accelerated or augmented. There are substantial differences across countries as well. Growth in China is now stronger than we projected both a year ago and in April 2009, but we have revised down by about 6 percentage points compared with a year ago the growth projections for two middle-income countries (Thailand and Malaysia) and by about 7 percentage points growth for two low-income countries (Cambodia and Mongolia).

Thanks to China, East Asia remains the fastest growing developing region in the world. Although China's economy accounts for less than a tenth of the global economy, the increase in China's GDP in 2009 will offset three-fourths of the decline in G3's GDP. This number underlies China's markedly increased global role, but also reveals the limits to what China alone can do, because this year's outcome was achieved through a huge monetary and fiscal stimulus that the authorities will find neither prudent nor necessary to sustain for an extended period of time. Take China out of the equation, however, and the remainder of the region is set to expand at a slower pace than the Middle East and North Africa, South Asia, and only modestly faster than Sub-Saharan Africa (Table 4). This reflects the openness of East Asia and the fast transmission of shocks through production networks serving the U.S., Japan and other global markets.

Figure 45. The increase in China's GDP offset three-fourths of the decline in G3's GDP

(in billions of dollars, 2009)

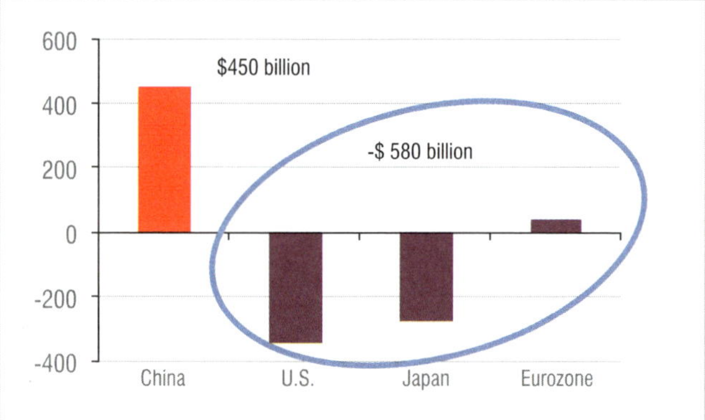

Source: World Bank.

Table 4. Thanks to China, developing East Asia will remain the fastest growing world region

(Percent change y-y)

	2007	2008	2009f	2010f
Developing East Asia	11.4	8.0	6.7	7.8
Dev. East Asia excl. China	6.2	4.8	1.1	4.5
Europe and Central Asia	7.1	4.3	-6.1	1.9
Latin America and Caribbean	5.5	3.9	-2.5	3.0
Middle East and North Africa	5.3	5.8	3.0	3.4
South Asia	8.5	5.7	5.3	6.4
Sub-Saharan Africa	6.5	4.9	0.7	3.8
OECD countries	2.5	0.4	-3.2	1.7

Sources: DECPG and World Bank staff estimates and projections.

China's economy will continue to influence substantially developments in the region in 2010. Real GDP growth is projected to strengthen modestly to 8.7 percent in 2010 from 8.4 percent in 2009, but the composition of growth is set to change significantly. Exports are projected to grow significantly after falling sharply in 2009, and real estate investment is bound to expand briskly. In 2010, the government stimulus is set to decline sharply. The authorities are committed not to withdraw any fiscal stimulus, but at the same time are mindful that substantial additional stimulus is also not warranted, given the strong growth prospects. Moreover, the extraordinary expansion in credit by the equivalent of 30 percent of GDP in 2009 could add to nonperforming loans (NPLs) in a repeat of the NPL accumulation during the 1990s. The government, as a result, may supplement the recently adopted measures to limit expansion in certain industries, including cement, steel and aluminum, with steps to slow rapid credit growth. This should also help address the authorities' growing concern about potential asset price bubbles.

Thailand and Malaysia are the region's middle-income countries worst hit by the crisis. In Thailand, a sharp decline in exports was the main cause for the economy to contract by 2.7 percent in 2009 amidst renewed political tensions. Prospects are for growth to recover in 2010 benefitting from inventory restocking and the pickup in demand for electronics and automobiles abroad. In Malaysia, the sharp drop in exports of oil, palm oil and electronics caused output to contract 2.3 percent this year.[11] The factors that battered the country on the downside are likely to support it as strongly on the upside, with increasing global demand, together with the positive effect from the second government stimulus package output projected to output to grow 4.1 percent in 2009.

Mongolia and Cambodia are the low-income countries hardest hit by the crisis. The collapse in copper prices hit Mongolia harder than the other major copper producers because of the country's particular combination of expansive fiscal and monetary policies, a fixed exchange rate and – at that time - an overheating financial sector. The government took strong actions to address the economic downturn from the start of 2009, supported by programs with the IMF, the World Bank, the ADB and Japan. These efforts have led to a stabilization of the external sector, the exchange rate and the budget, although nonperforming loans are still rising. Real GDP growth is projected to slow from nearly 9 percent in 2008 to 0.5 percent in 2009 before recovering modestly in 2010. The slowdown in economic activity in Cambodia is as sharp, with real GDP projected to contract 2 percent in 2009 after expanding nearly 7 percent in 2008. Exports of garments – which account for the bulk of shipments abroad and are almost all directed to the U.S. market - fell 26 percent in the first six months of 2009 from a year earlier. More worrisome than the decline in garment exports, however, is the loss in U.S. market share that indicates competitiveness challenges. The other key sectors of the economy were also negatively affected. Tourism arrivals declined and construction projects approved dropped one-fourth from a year before in the first half of the year. As in Mongolia, developments in the banking sector bear close watch. Very rapid growth

11 Malaysia's value added contribution to electronics exports is the highest in the region.

over 2005-2008 has slowed to a halt, while non-performing loans have increased during the first six months of 2009 and will be under further pressure because of economic weakness and the sharp downward correction in real estate prices.

Looking beyond next year, East Asia has the potential to sustain high growth rates even in a more slowly growing global economy, but such an outcome will require substantial policy efforts. Until recently, some of the economies in the region strived to achieve rapid growth by imitating the earlier policies in Japan; Taiwan, China; and Korea of relying on export-led manufacturing growth, often without full regard for the costs and distortions incurred in the process. At the heart of these policies were undervalued exchange rates, accompanied with government measures to encourage the rapid build-up of manufacturing capacity for export, while boosting domestic saving, depressing household consumption and limiting competition, both domestic and foreign, in the nontradeable sectors. Favorable tax, customs and credit policies benefitting large export-oriented companies have been essential, as have been efforts to create the necessary facilitating infrastructure and conditions for attracting foreign investors in export-oriented sectors.

Figure 46. Domestically unbalanced: private consumption in the U.S. and China

(In percent of GDP)

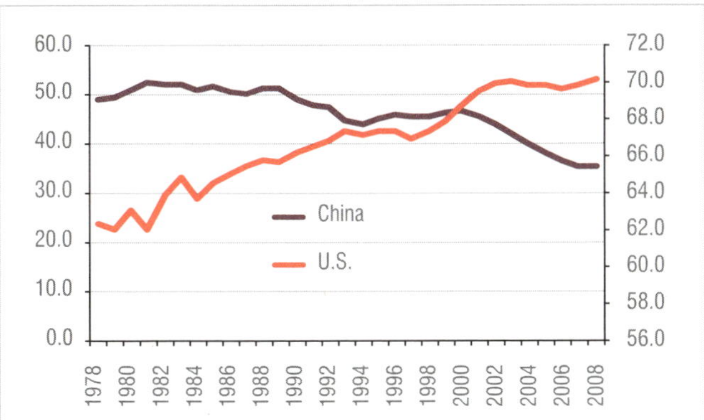

Sources: Datastream and BEA.

First among the countries in developing East Asia, the authorities in China began to recognize that the investment-heavy, industry-led pattern of export-led manufacturing growth pursued over the last three decades has led to unsustainable domestic and external imbalances (Figure 46). The Chinese authorities remain committed to rebalancing growth as the key objective in its 11th five-year plan by giving greater attention to domestic sources of growth, increasing the role of services and consumption, improving energy efficiency, encouraging environmental sustainability, and reducing urban-rural inequalities. In this context, further reform of energy prices is one of the government's priorities, and carrying it forward will bring more starkly into focus the important question of reforming other relative prices, including interest rates and the exchange rate. The current crisis arguably slowed progress in rebalancing, as the authorities focused on limiting the slowdown in growth by implementing the 4 trillion RMB infrastructure-dominated fiscal stimulus package and effectively re-pegging the currency to the U.S. dollar. Nonetheless, senior Chinese leaders have stressed that the crisis makes rebalancing more urgent and important. Several measures to support private consumption have been undertaken thus far this year, including tax breaks for automobile purchases and subsidies for electronics sales, increases in pensions, the rolling out of a rural pension program, and the start of an important health reform program. These measures are helping sustain growth in private consumption in 2009 at a pace little changed from last year, modestly boosting the share of consumption in GDP. Nonetheless, significantly more efforts will be needed towards rebalancing, particularly in the area of removing the distortions that have kept growth in services, wages and private consumption lower than growth in overall GDP.

Other developing East Asian countries are also likely to explore ways for extracting more growth from domestic demand while recognizing that developing countries will need to increase integration with global goods and service markets to sustain convergence with high-income economies. Observers point out that Vietnam faces challenges not very different from those faced by China, given the similarity of growth models pursued thus far. Malaysia and Thailand are striving to avoid the middle income trap, including by focusing on improving education and skills, tackling infrastructure bottlenecks, and enhancing competition in

Figure 47. Not all countries have subdued private consumption as in China

(Private consumption, in percent of GDP, 2008)

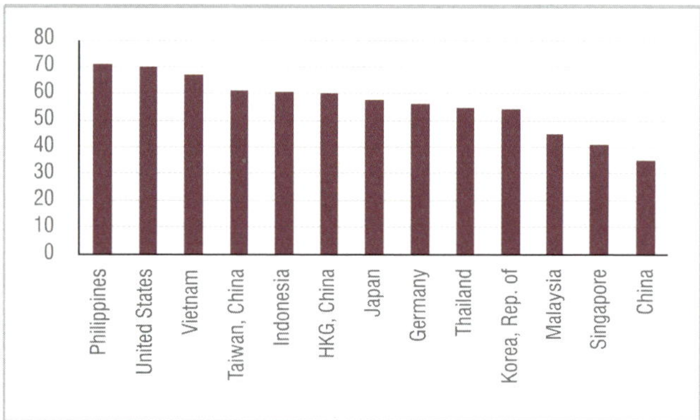

Sources: Datastream and national authorities.

Figure 48. The service sector is much smaller in China and Indonesia than in countries at similar income levels

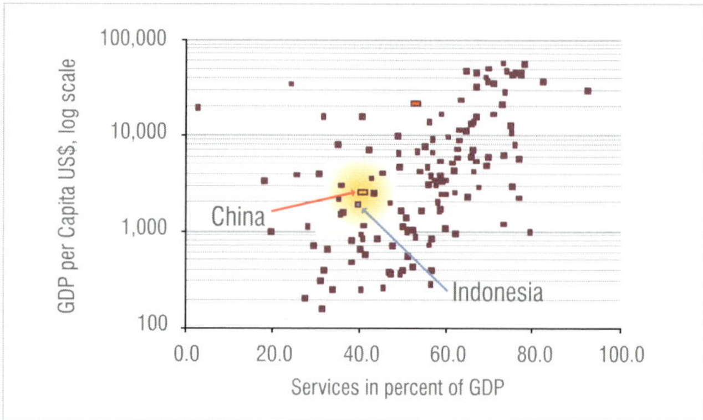

Sources: Datastream, Haver and World Bank staff estimates.

both the manufacturing and the service sectors. Malaysia's recent measures and announcements to liberalize the service sector and promote private investment, research and development and new niche areas are important first steps in this regard but would have greater impact if followed by further reforms in the regulatory framework.

In contrast to these countries, the authorities in the Philippines and some of the low-income countries face a different challenge. In the Philippines, the level of household consumption relative to income is similar to that in the U.S. and is much higher than in other countries in the region, fueled by strong inflows of remittances (Figure 47). Capital-intensive production of goods and services, meanwhile, is predominantly inward-oriented and the value-added of exports is lower than in the other middle-income countries in the region. Transforming the economy by increasing its outward orientation will remain an important challenge for the government (see below).

East Asia's process of regional integration – that followed the global integration of most countries – has been a powerful driver of growth in the region. Although advanced, the process of regional integration could be deepened substantially further by addressing behind-the-border trade facilitation problems, tackling the liberalization of the services sector, including the financial sector (see below), and facilitating intra-regional migration. Harmonizing infrastructure and improving policy transparency are also important avenues for the authorities to explore. Global and regional production networks, along with the rapid rise in intra-regional trade in parts and components, have further room for growth and improvement, although some point out that higher energy prices in the future and concerns about climate change may lead to a rethink of the level of specialization and intra-industry trade which may place limits on economies of scale in manufacturing. Moving up the value-added chain in production networks will give growth a new impetus, as the benefits of new technology and innovation spread more broadly throughout the countries in the region.

The service sector – underdeveloped in many East Asian countries due to the bias in favor of merchandise tradeables – holds enormous potential for the region. Removing barriers to the development of the service sector needs to be pursued with sufficient urgency in countries such as China, Malaysia, Korea and Thailand where the need for finding new sources of growth is becoming crucial given the likelihood that import demand in developed countries is set to remain weak and where the limits of traditional growth strategies as vehicles of reaching high income status are being tested. Efforts need to include the reduction and elimination of tax incentives in favor of export-oriented manufacturing, opening up the service sector to more competition, including from foreign investors, and helping improve the access to finance for small- and medium-size enterprises. Easing restrictions to internal migration in China and advancing reforms to limit preferential treatment of different classes of citizens in other countries should offer substantial scope for increasing urban employment, raising household incomes, and allowing for better use of agglomeration

Figure 49. The share of services in GDP has risen along with incomes per capita in Korea */

(In percent)

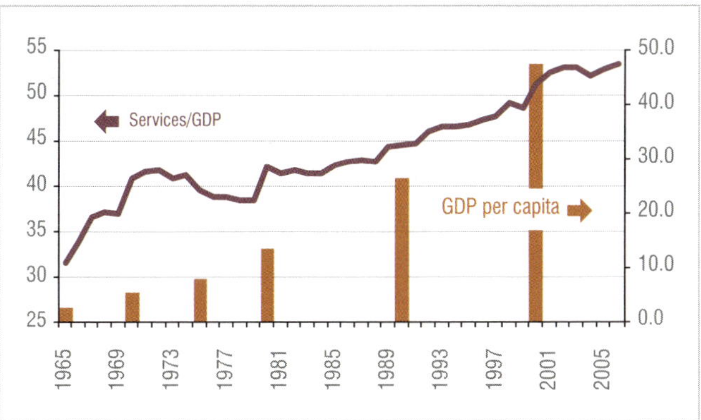

Sources: WDI, OECD and Haver Analytics. Note: */GDP per capita is in current U.S. dollars relative to the U.S.

Figure 50. Philippines: service employment denominates

(In percent of total)

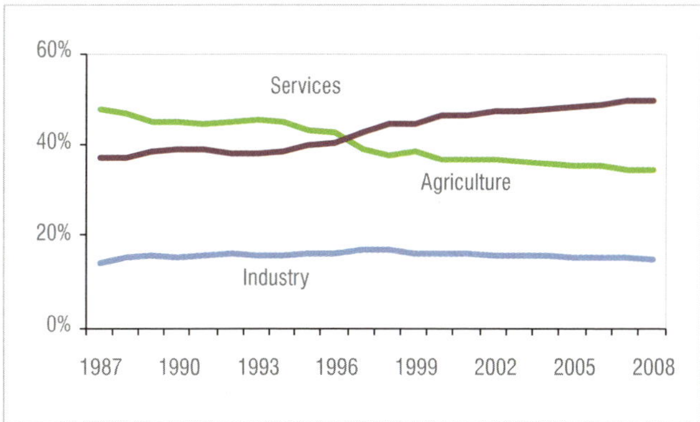

Source: Philippines growth brief prepared by Ulrich Lachler, World Bank, based on data from the national authorities.

economies. In Korea, the authorities are rightly concerned that labor productivity in the service sector – dominated by SMEs – has expanded by just about 1 percent a year this decade, six times slower than manufacturing productivity, largely due to the financial difficulties among SMEs in accessing finance, dealing with business regulation and labor market rigidities.

Consider the potential of the service sector for China. Value-added in services accounts for 40 percent of GDP, below the midpoint of the range for countries with broadly similar income per capita (25-75 percent) and the same as in Indonesia (a country with half of China's income per capita). Indeed, the share of value-added in services in China has risen modestly from 32 percent of GDP in 1960, when GDP per capita was substantially lower. In Korea, services accounted for about 40 percent of GDP in the mid-1970s when GDP per capita was the same as China's level today relative to the U.S. The share of services has risen to about 50 percent subsequently, measured in current prices. As emphasized above, development of the service sector in Korea has been restrained by policies geared toward export-led goods manufacturing and this is an important similarity with China. Nonetheless, services accounted for half of the increase in real GDP in Korea over the last 25 years, or a contribution equivalent to that of the rest of the economy. An ambitious agenda for developing the service sector in China, therefore, could help boost output, employment and living standards well beyond current projections.

In contrast to China and Indonesia, the service sector in the Philippines is large but that reflects a failure to boost economic activity more generally, rather than a mark of success in diversifying the structure of growth. The Philippines was the most developed country in developing Asia in the 1950s, but subpar rates of growth, coupled with policies protecting inefficient manufacturing based on excessively capital-intensive technology in the subsequent three decades, caused living standards to stagnate to levels that are now below all other middle-income countries in the region. Industry was unable to absorb the rapidly growing labor force, including migrants from the rural areas, leaving the service sector as the safety valve. Services account for 65 percent of GDP and nearly half of employment, but anecdotal evidence suggests that the bulk of the service sector simply masks severe urban underemployment with very low productivity. A ray of hope has been offered by the success of the Business Process Outsourcing (BPO) service sector, which in less than a decade has risen as a formidable global competitor to companies in India – still the preferred destination for BPO. More will need to be done to help the BPO boost employment from 1 percent of the total in the country, however, and policies to be pursued will also facilitate the emergence of other higher value-added and high productivity services and manufacturing.

There are both downside and upside risks to the outlook presented in this report. On the downside, the main risk is that private investment and consumption in developed countries remain very weak because of sizable excess capacity and high unemployment, keeping overall growth in the advanced economies dependent on sustaining for an extended period of time fiscal and monetary

Figure 51. Global imbalances have been reduced – but not by Asia

(absolute value of current account balances, in percent of global GDP)

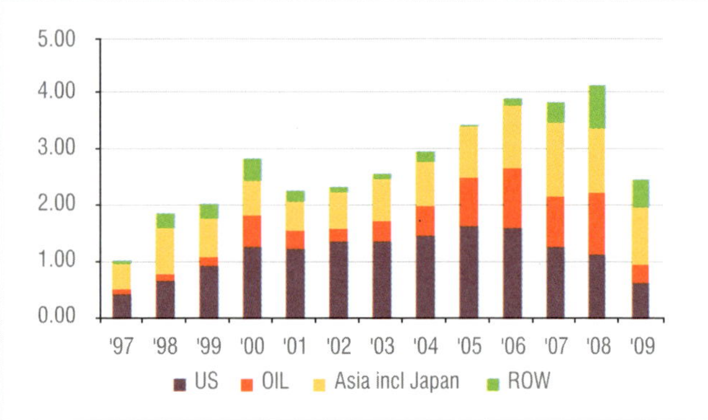

Sources: Datastream and national authorities.

Figure 52. The share of foreign exchange reserves denominated in dollars has eased only slowly

(In percent)

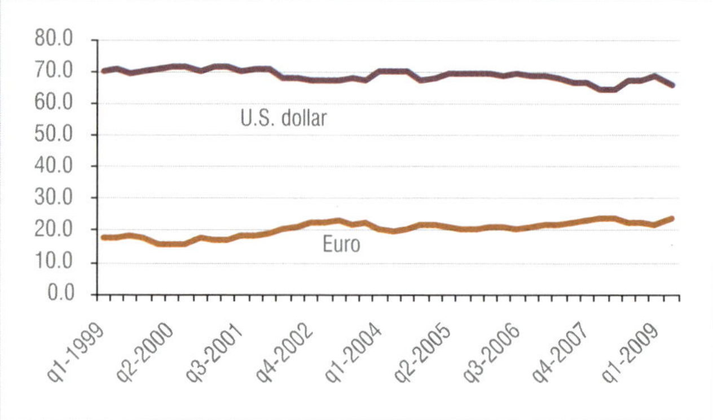

Source: IMF.

stimulus. The authorities, as a result, may face the unpalatable choice of whether to keep up the stimulus at greater risks to fiscal sustainability and developed country currencies, or withdraw it and risk a double dip in economic activity. Even if stimulus is sustained, the risk is that the crisis has triggered a more permanent shift to lower potential growth for the developed countries. Such economic developments will give rise to populist and protectionist sentiment in developed and developing countries alike. Finally, continued problems with financial institutions that have yet to realize more than half of likely losses could also trigger another round of financial instability.

The upside risks are substantial as well. A more robust recovery in the developed countries than currently expected could come before global imbalances are tackled more vigorously and financial regulation in advanced economies improved to rein in the excesses that led to the crisis. Such a recovery will likely put East Asia under strong pressure to return to the status quo ante of supporting manufacturing exports at any cost. The upside also carries with it the risk that East Asia's growth potential and much improved financial markets attract larger capital inflows than assumed under the baseline scenario, leading to new and larger asset price bubbles and complicating macroeconomic policies. Managing both the upside and the downside risks will be a challenge to any government. Rebalancing growth, together with advancing integration with global markets and retooling institutions to encourage innovation however, seems to be the key ingredient of any strategy to tackle the problems the next two years will bring to policymakers in the region.

The crisis accelerated the process of reducing global current account imbalances but it is unclear if progress will be sustained. The U.S. current account deficit peaked in 2006 at 6 percent of GDP (1.6 percent of global GDP) and was declining even before the crisis began, as the weak dollar helped slow growth in imports more than exports (Figure 51). Surpluses among the oil producers peaked in 2008 along with oil prices. The current account surplus in East Asia (developing East Asia, the NIEs and Japan), by contrast, has narrowed only modestly in 2009 from the 2008 peak. Continued dollar weakness, reflecting improved confidence in the rest of the world – notably in East Asia – and increased worries about the potential difficulties in reducing the U.S. fiscal deficits that are set to average 10 percent of GDP in the fiscal years 2009 and 2010, holds the potential of reducing imbalances further in the near term. A lot will depend, however, whether the dollar will weaken against a broader basket of currencies, notably the currencies of the countries with the largest surpluses.

But currency appreciation cannot be a goal in itself. Allowing currencies in the region to strengthen, but by no more than differential labor productivity growth in the tradeable sectors, will help rebalance the economy gradually and improve living standards without endangering competitiveness. Most authorities in the region nonetheless worry that appreciation will stymie the potential recovery in exports in the short term, while encouraging capital inflows that would bring instability to financial systems and exert further upward pressure on currencies. The authorities in many East Asian countries, moreover, are concerned about losing competitiveness against China, should they allow their currencies to strengthen at a time when China has effectively re-pegged the renminbi to the weakening dollar since mid-2008. Some observers have suggested that if such concerns persist, countries in the region may consider intervening jointly to appreciate their currencies against the dollar in a move similar to the Louvre Accord signed in 1987 to stem the depreciation of the U.S. dollar.[12] The likelihood of such a development does not appear high at present, however.

Over the longer term, the likely sustained shift in global economic power to East Asia, notably to China, will play an increasingly larger role in shaping the available options of reserve currencies. The firming multi-polarity in the world economic order in the aftermath of the recent global crisis has led some to question the role of the U.S. dollar as the world's predominant reserve currency. The dollar's share of global foreign exchange reserves was trending modestly down before the global financial crisis intensified with the failure of Lehman Brothers, but demand for short-term U.S. government bonds surged at the height of the crisis even as their yields fell essentially to zero. A renewed shift away from the dollar has been evident again from the start of 2009, supported by returning confidence in the rest of the world and concerns that U.S. fiscal deficits of about 10 percent of GDP in 2009 and 2010 and government debt up by about 25 percent of GDP by 2011 will dampen prospects for the U.S. currency (Figure 52).

What options are there for global reserve currencies in the future? Demand for the euro as a reserve currency may increase somewhat further over the medium term, but observers note that the currency's position will be limited as long as the eurozone lacks a single euro-bond market and a single eurozone finance authority. Officials from the BRIC countries have recently proposed a greater role for both the SDR and their own currencies. The general IMF SDR allocation in August injected the equivalent of $250 billion into the global economy and gave rise to much of the discussion about using the synthetic currency as an alternative reserve currency. The allocation amounted to just 3 percent of global foreign exchange reserves, however. There may be a role for the SDR in a global reserve system, but it must be supported by improved governance arrangements, along the lines articulated at the recent G20 Summit in Pittsburgh. The Chinese authorities, meanwhile, have begun work to encourage the use of the renminbi in trade settlements with trading partners, and promoting its financial centers, including Hong Kong, China, with the ultimate goal of making the currency convertible and elevating it to global reserve currency status. Such ambitions are underpinned by the likelihood that even with slower growth than recorded in recent years, China's GDP is likely to exceed that of the U.S. in about 25 years – and Japan's perhaps in as few as five.[13] All in all, these factors make it more likely that a multi-polar reserve currency world will emerge over the longer term and, if supplemented with stronger global economic cooperation as pledged at the G20 Summit in Pittsburgh, could ultimately limit the need for countries to hold ever larger foreign exchange reserves to self insure against unfavorable external shocks.[14]

The November G20 Summit in Pittsburgh acknowledged the need to sustain strong policy responses until a durable recovery is secured, and stressed yet again the need for continued policy coordination and consultation to tackle global imbalances and improve regulatory frameworks that are understood to be among the primary causes of the crisis. The authorities in the region are mindful of the risks of a premature withdrawal of stimulus before recovery of private investment is on a sound footing. Some

12 The signing of the Louvre Accord by the G-7 (other than Italy) followed the Plaza Accord in 1985 which aimed to weaken the dollar against the DM and the Japanese yen.

13 Assuming real GDP growth in China exceeds that in the U.S. by 5.5 percentage points, for example, 8 percent growth in China and 2.5 percent real GDP growth in the U.S.

14 Also see the discussion in Mansoor Dailami and Paul Masson, 2009, The Multipolar International Monetary System, manuscript.

governments in the region will have the fiscal space to sustain fiscal stimulus until the transition from a rebound to a recovery is ensured, while others will be more fiscally constrained. Nonetheless, even those with ample room for fiscal maneuver are aware that fiscal and monetary policy alone cannot ensure a return to the levels of production that prevailed before the crisis if, as it seems likely, developed countries will recover only slowly.

COUNTRY PAGES & KEY INDICATORS

CAMBODIA

Population	14 million
Population growth	1.7 percent
Surface area	181,000 sq.km.
Capital	Phnom Penh

Cambodia's economy is contracting in 2009 and is expected to recover slowly in 2010. Through large trade flows – mainly in garments and services – and large inflows of foreign investment, Cambodia was very exposed to the global economic crisis. Although the country had a sound fiscal position and built international reserves, weak revenue mobilization and pervasive dollarization have constrained the policy reaction to the external shocks. Fiscal loosening in 2009 is supporting the economy, although it is creating tensions for macroeconomic management. Intensive bank supervision is also critical, as the banking sector faces the negative consequences of lower economic growth and much lower real estate prices.

Real GDP is projected to contract 2 percent in 2009 from nearly 7 percent in 2008 and four years of double digit growth before that. Agriculture, accounting for 27 percent of GDP, is the bright spot, with continued improvement in paddy rice production despite irregular rains in 2009. Exports of garments – which account for the bulk of shipments abroad and are almost all directed to the U.S. market - fell 26 percent in the first six months of 2009 from a year earlier. The loss of market share in the U.S. market, from 3.2 last year to 2.8 percent in mid-2009 is an equally worrisome development, indicating competitiveness challenges. The other key sectors of the economy were also negatively affected. Tourism arrivals declined and construction projects approved dropped one-fourth from a year before in the first half of the year.

There are initial signs of recovery leading to 4 percent real GDP growth in 2010. Construction might be bottoming out, reflecting new capital inflows. Hotel bookings are also improving, although tentatively. There are, however, signs of corporate stress. Access to finance – from domestic banks or foreign investment – remains subdued. New firm registration has plummeted 40 percent from a year earlier in the first 6 months of 2009, and 18 percent of garment factories have closed (net of opening), with a number of others under severe liquidity. Household debt has also increased under the pressure of higher prices in 2008 and lower income in 2009. Such corporate and household vulnerability will weaken the pace of recovery.

The current account deficit is being reduced in 2009 but the accumulation of foreign exchange reserves has slowed. The fall in garment exports and tourism revenues has been more than offset by the fall in imports of inputs for garments and tourism and the lower price of petroleum products. As a result, the current account deficit (excluding official transfers) has decreased during the first six months from $748 million to $643 million in 2009, with a projected deficit of 9.9 percent of GDP in 2009. The financing of the deficit has correspondingly decreased, with foreign investment over the first six months decreasing from $486 million to $223 million. The current account deficit is projected to widen modestly in 2010, as a rebound in domestic demand and oil prices boosts imports.

Exchange market intervention by the central bank to limit depreciation of the domestic currency and maintain the riel around 4,100 per U.S. dollar has slowed growth in foreign exchange reserves this year. Still, reserves rose modestly from a year earlier to $2.2 billion by the end of June 2009. Cambodia's real effective exchange rate appreciated 2-3 percent in June 2009 from a year earlier. Prices are down 4.9 percent in June from a year before, reflecting the sharp downward correction

Garment industry: exports and workers

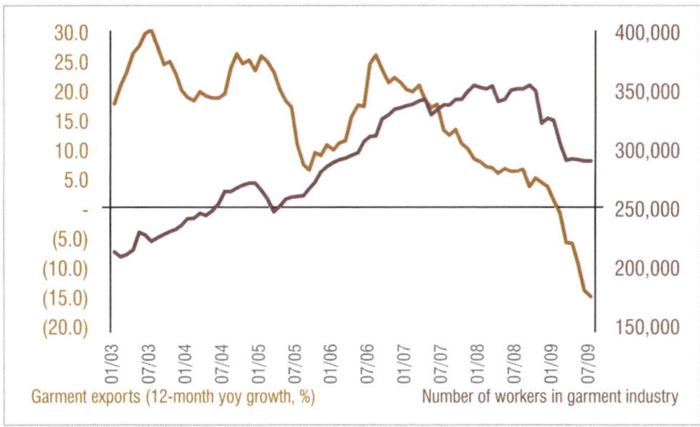

in food and fuel prices. Upward pressures on inflation might reemerge as international prices of commodities rebound and as depreciation pressures continue. The monetary policy has been appropriately eased early 2009.

Developments in the banking sector bear close watch. Very rapid growth over 2005-2008 has stretched the risk management and supervisory capacity. The liquidity situation has significantly improved since late 2008, but at the cost of high deposits rates to mobilize savings, putting pressure on bank profitability. The non-performing loans ratio has increased during the first six months of 2009 and will be under further pressure as the deceleration in the economy and the deflation of the real estate bubble impact loan performance. Credit to private sector remains weak, with year-on-year growth at only 10 percent at the end of June

Cambodia: Key Indicators

	2004	2005	2006	2007	2008	2009e	2010f
Output, Employment and Prices							
Real GDP (% change y-y)	10.3	13.3	10.8	10.2	6.7	-2.2	4.2
Industrial production index (2000=100)	170.1	191.7	226.7	245.7	255.7	229.9	234.5
(% change y-y)	16.6	12.7	18.3	8.4	4.1	-10.1	2.0
Unemployment (%)	1.0	..	..	..	..	..	..
Consumer price index (% change y-y)	5.3	8.4	4.2	14.0	12.5	3.5	5.0
Public Sector							
Government balance (% GDP)	-4.6	-2.5	-2.7	-2.9	-2.8	-6.7	-6.0
Foreign Trade, BOP and External Debt							
Trade balance (millions US$)	-681	-1,018	-1,078	-1,382	-1,826	-1,646	-2,284
Exports of goods (millions US$)	2,589	2,910	3,693	4,089	4,708	3,908	4,103
(% change y-y)	24.1	12.4	26.9	10.7	15.2	-17.0	5.0
Key export (% change y-y) 1/	23.2	10.5	21.1	8.1	3.3	-20.0	1.0
Imports of goods (millions US$)	3,270	3,928	4,771	5,471	6,534	5,554	6,387
(% change y-y)	22.5	20.1	21.5	14.7	19.4	-15.0	15.0
Current account balance (millions US$) 2/	-435	-606	-522	-705	-1716	-1100	-1,700
(% GDP)	-8.2	-9.7	-7.1	-8.1	-15.4	-10.2	-14.1
Foreign direct investment (millions US$)	121	375	475	866	815	510	725.0
External debt (millions US$)	3,080	3,155	3,318	3,537	3,892	2,450	2,590
(% GDP)	57.9	50.4	45.1	40.4	34.8	22.7	21.6
Short-term debt (millions US$)	262	279	209	218	218	218	217.8
Debt service (% exports of g&s)	2.1	1.8	1.4	9.0	0.9	1.0	1.2
Foreign exchange reserves (millions US$)	809	915	1,097	1,616	2,164	2,200	2,200
(months of imports of g&s)	2.6	2.4	2.4	3.0	3.4	4.0	3.5
Financial Markets							
Domestic credit (% change y-y)	33.0	22.6	35.7	70.7	51.1	15.0	18.0
Short-term interest rate (% p.a.) 3/	16.7	16.2	16.4	16.0	15.8	15.0	14.5
Exchange rate (Riel/US$, eop)	4031	4116	4061	4003	4081	4165	..
Real effective exchange rate (2000=100)	91.5	95.9	94.3	99.2	112.8	111.5	..
(% change y-y)	-0.8	4.9	-1.7	5.2	13.7	-1.2	..
Memo: Nominal GDP (millions US$)	5,318	6,257	7,350	8,753	11,170	10,811	12,015

Sources: National data sources and World Bank staff estimates.
e = estimate
f = forecast
1/ Garments
2/ Excludes official transfers
3/ One-year US$ loans

2009. An overdraft facility has been created in early 2009 to address liquidity issues and new regulations have been passed to strengthen banking supervision.

The fiscal deficit is expected to expand to 6.7 percent of GDP, beyond the budget target of 4 percent, largely because of larger than budgeted spending. Despite the extension of tax cuts in response to the crisis and the sharper downturn, the annual revenue target is expected to be met. The larger increase in spending, meanwhile, reflects mainly a larger wage bill. While the mobilization of foreign assistance is on track, it is not sufficient to finance the wider deficit. The government, as a result, is drawing down its deposits (budget reserves built up over the past few years, thanks to progress in public financial management and prudent fiscal policy).

The government is facing difficult choices in drafting the 2010 budget. Sustaining high deficits that exceed available external financing would put pressure on macroeconomic stability. Hence the government is trying to bring the fiscal deficit to a level that supports growth – which remains below potential – without compromising macroeconomic stability.

Beyond the policy mix (including fiscal measures), a number of policy reforms are being taken to respond to the global economic crisis. A number of trade and investment treaties have been signed, including through ASEAN. Cambodia now enjoys preferential access to "everything but arms" in the European Union. A National Arbitration Center will soon be established. Trade facilitation reforms and investment promotion efforts are ongoing.

The impact of the crisis on Cambodians' livelihoods is deemed significant but varies across the population. Only one-fifth of all households have a job in sectors directly affected by the crisis (garments, construction, and tourism). Urban households and richer households are more likely to be affected through these sectors, but the income impact is greatest amongst poorer and rural households, for whom these jobs, if present, account for a far larger share of income. Projections suggest that the crisis could add 1 to 4 percentage points to the poverty headcount between 2007 and 2010. The key challenge ahead is whether the economy can absorb new labor entrants as well as labor shed from crisis-affected sectors. Compounding these vulnerabilities are high levels of debt for a number of households and the fact that the slowdown comes on the heels of soaring food prices in 2007 (which had a major distributional impact, and probably adverse effects on poverty). There is currently limited data on human development outcomes, but preliminary indications and experience in other countries suggest that the impact will be a reversal of the very encouraging trends of the past decade.

CHINA

Population	1,318 million
Population growth	0.6 percent
Surface area	9,598,000 sq.km.
Capital	Beijing

Exceptionally large fiscal and monetary stimulus has supported a strong recovery in China's economy despite the large drag on growth from exports amidst the global recession. Reflecting a large increase in domestic demand, real GDP growth surged to 8.9 percent year-on-year in the third quarter from a low of 6.1 percent in the first. China's stimulus policies included a discretionary fiscal stimulus of perhaps 3.5 percent of GDP and a surge in bank lending that may reach 30 percent of GDP in 2009. Most of the stimulus has shown up in infrastructure-oriented government-influenced investment. However some of the stimulus has been consumption-oriented and the acceleration in domestic demand has been more broad-based. Resurgent housing sales have started to feed through to construction activity. Consumption held up well, even as it lagged investment. However, other market based investment in several sectors, notably manufacturing, is affected by spare capacity. Export volumes fell 16 percent from a year earlier in the first three quarters of 2009. The fall in exports has been very broad-based, geographically and in terms of products. With net exports of goods and services subtracting the equivalent of 3.7 percentage points from GDP growth in January-September.

The current account surplus has declined. Larger imports of raw materials—which made up almost one-half of non-processing imports in 2008—have been the key driver of import growth in 2009. Imports of machinery and equipment have also been robust. With overall imports holding up much better than exports, the trade surplus declined 25 percent in January-September from a year earlier in dollar terms and the current account surplus has declined from 9.8 percent of GDP in 2008 to 6.4 percent of GDP in the first half of 2009. Exchange market intervention has boosted foreign exchange reserves sharply higher this year to about $2.3 trillion.

The slowdown has had a major impact on the labor market. Many jobs have been shed, particularly in export-oriented manufacturing sectors. The domestic economy has created new jobs at the same time, largely in services and the government sector, and overall conditions on the labor market are not as bad as feared earlier this year. Nonetheless, significant numbers of people have had to accept wage cuts. These labor market trends have put downward pressure on general wage growth, particularly in the more flexible segments of the labor market. Migrant wage income growth "per capita" slowed to 7.6 percent in January-June 2009 from a year earlier.

Real GDP growth in 2009 is likely to exceed the government target of 8 percent of GDP, and the pace of activity will probably strengthen in 2010. But the composition of growth will change in 2010, with the increase in exports likely to be significant, supported by strong fundamental competitiveness and the recent depreciation of the RMB in nominal effective terms (as the RMB was effectively pegged to the US dollar since mid-2008). Thus, net exports are likely to stop being a drag on growth. Real estate investment is also bound to be stronger. However, the government stimulus is set to decline sharply next year. Market based investment is likely to continue to feel pressure from spare capacity, while consumption may feel some headwind from the weaker labor market situation. All in all, we expect GDP growth to rise somewhat in 2010, but a sharper acceleration is not likely until the global economy recovers more fully. In this climate, inflation pressures are expected to remain low.

Real GDP growth

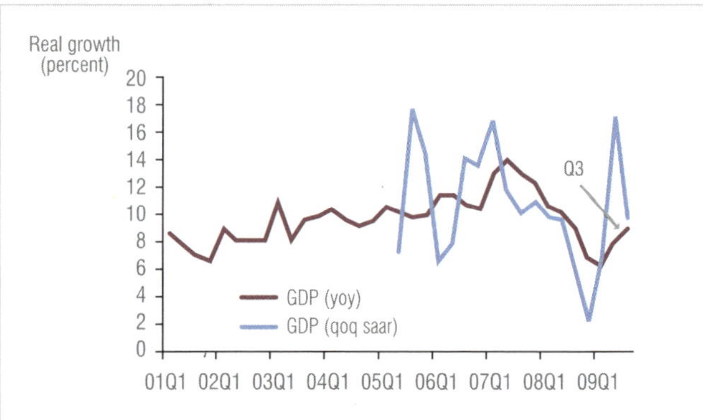

China: Key Indicators

	2006	2007	2008	2009e	2010f	2008	2009			2009			
	Year	Year	Year	Year	Year	Q4	Q1	Q2	Q3	Jun	Jul	Aug	Sep
Output, Employment and Prices													
Real GDP (% change y-y)	11.6	13.0	9.0	8.4	8.7	6.8	6.1	7.9	8.9	..	..	..	..
Industrial production index /1	..	..	..	..		..	..	..		..	..	..	..
(% change y-y)	12.9	14.9	9.5	9.0	9.0	6.4	5.3	9.0	12.3	10.7	10.8	12.3	13.9
Unemployment (%) 2/	4.1	4.0	4.2	4.3	4.3	4.2	4.3	4.3	4.3	4.3	4.3	4.3	4.3
Real wages (% change y-y)	12.7	13.6	11.0	..	..	12.2	14.1	14.1	16.4	..	..	..	..
Consumer price index (% change y-y)	1.5	4.8	5.9	-0.2	1.5	2.5	-0.6	-1.5	-1.3	-1.7	-1.8	-1.2	-0.8
Public Sector													
Government balance (% GDP)	-1.0	0.6	-0.4	-3.3	-4.1	..	..	..	..	..	..	..	..
Domestic public sector debt (% GDP) /3	19.7	26.0	24.5	19.4	21.8	..	..	..	..	..	..	..	..
Foreign Trade, BOP and External Debt													
Trade balance (billions US$)	177.5	262.5	296.5	226.0	229.0	114.3	62.6	35.1	39.4	8.5	10.8	15.7	12.9
Exports of goods (billions US$)	969.3	1218.3	1428.5	1128.0	1201.0	354.5	245.7	276.4	325.1	95.6	105.5	103.7	115.9
(% change y-y) 4/	27.2	25.7	17.3	-21.0	6.5	4.3	-19.7	-23.3	-20.3	-21.4	-22.8	-23.4	-15.2
Key export (% change y-y) 5/	28.5	26.2	16.8	-21.5	6.8	4.1	-19.7	-23.2	-20.1	-20.6	-22.5	-22.9	-14.9
Imports of goods (billions US$)	791.8	955.8	1132.0	902.0	972.0	240.2	183.1	241.3	285.7	87.1	94.7	88.0	103.0
(% change y-y) 4/	19.9	20.7	18.4	-20.3	7.8	-8.9	-30.8	-20.4	-12.0	-13.2	-14.9	-17.0	-3.5
Current account balance (billions US$)	253.3	371.8	426.0	254.0	207.0	..	..	..	..	..	..	..	..
(% GDP)	9.5	11.0	9.8	5.4	4.1	..	..	..	..	..	..	..	..
Foreign direct investment (billions US$) /6	72.7	83.5	108.3	84.0	102.0	108.3	21.8	43.0	63.8				
External debt (billions US$)	325.3	373.8	378.2	340.6	309.0	..	..	..	..	..	..	..	..
(% GDP)	12.2	11.1	8.7	7.1	5.8	..	..	..	..	..	..	..	..
Short-term debt (billions US$)	173.4	203.7	187.2	187.0	187.0	..	..	..	..	..	..	..	..
Debt service (% exports of g&s)	2.1	2.0	2.2	1.9	1.7	..	..	..	..	..	..	..	..
Foreign exchange reserves (billions US$)	1074	1533	1950	2376	2610	1952	1960	2138	2279	2138	2181	2217	2279
(months of imports of g&s)	16.3	19.2	19.6	25.8	28.8	24.4	32.1	26.6	23.9	2.0	1.9	2.1	1.8
Financial Markets													
Domestic credit (% change y-y)	15.7	16.1	15.9	30.0	17.6	18.8	29.8	34.4	34.2	34.4	34.0	34.0	34.2
Short-term interest rate (% p.a.) 7/	3.3	3.3	2.8	3.0	3.3	2.8	2.8	2.8	2.8	2.8	2.8	2.8	2.8
Exchange rate (RMB/US$, eop)	7.82	7.37	6.84	6.76	6.62	6.84	6.83	6.83	6.83	6.83	6.83	6.83	6.8
Real effective exchange rate (2000=100)	102.2	103.6	118.1	..	..	121.2	124.7	116.4	116.5	116.4	116.0	117.1	116.5
(% change y-y)	-1.8	1.3	13.9	..	..	12.9	15.3	5.8	-1.7	7.4	6.6	3.2	-0.7
Stock market index (Dec. 19, 1990=100)/8	2676	5262	1821	..	..	1821	2373	2959	2779	2959	3412	2668	2779
Memo: Nominal GDP (billions US$)	2,658	3,382	4,327	4,786	5,349	..	..	..	..	..	..	..	..

Source: National data sources

f = forecast

1/ Annual data are not comparable with the quarterly and monthly data. Annual data cover all industrial enterprises while the quarterly and monthly ones only refer to those enterprises with sales value above Rmb5 millions.

2/ Official urban unemployment only, not including laid-off workers

3/ Includes treasury bond, policy financial bond and other financial bond (end-period outstanding)

4/ Nominal growth rate

5/ Manufactured exports

6/ Gross FDI utilized

7/ Central Bank loans to financial institutions, less than 20 days

8/ Shanghai Stock Exchange A-Share Price Composite

China's external surplus is set to shrink sharply this year and remain broadly unchanged in 2010. We project a current account surplus of around 5.5 percent of GDP for 2009 as a whole. In 2010, with domestic demand expected to remain robust and processing trade recovering, overall imports should continue to grow solidly. With exports projected to grow at broadly the same pace as imports, and terms of trade likely to remain little changed after this year's improvement, the current account surplus will remain roughly unchanged. Over the medium term, with the gap between domestic growth in China and the rest of the world is likely to diminish, leading to further widening of the surplus even if China's pattern of growth is rebalanced successfully.

Looking ahead, the costs and risks of sustaining the current expansionary policy stance will increase over time. The government intends to keep the overall macroeconomic policy stance broadly unchanged for now. In our view, macroeconomic conditions in the real economy do indeed not call for a major tightening. However, risks of asset price bubbles and misallocation of resources amidst abundant liquidity need to be mitigated and monetary policy will have to be tightened sooner than in developed countries. In the fiscal area, significant additional stimulus does not seem warranted, although additional flexibility will be needed.

The recovery can only be sustained by successful rebalancing of the economy. Rebalancing and getting more growth out of the domestic economy call for more emphasis on consumption and services and less on investment and industry. Following on earlier initiatives, some steps have been taken in recent months to rebalance and boost domestic demand. Recent steps include increasing the presence of the government in health, education, and social safety, including the rolling out of a rural pension program and implementing elements of the health care reform plan announced earlier this year; improving access to finance and SME development; and mitigating resource use and environmental damage, notably by coupling domestic fuel prices to the international oil price and increases in water prices and some electricity tariffs. Regionally, government-led investment has been emphasized in poorer regions away from the coastal areas. These are useful steps, although more policy measures will be needed to rebalance growth in China, given the underlying strong momentum of the existing pattern.

FIJI

Population	834 million
Population growth	0.5 percent
Surface area	18,000 sq.km.
Capital	Suva

Weaker demand abroad combined with the January floods have affected negatively economic activity. In January 2009, the biggest floods in forty years devastated the west coast of Fiji's main island and disrupted power supply, damaged crop fields and infrastructure, and limited tourist arrivals. Preliminary estimates suggest that the direct costs of the floods on the economy amount to about $180 million (5¼ percent of GDP). The government projects output to contract 0.3 percent in 2009 after an expansion of 0.2 percent in 2008, but a larger decline is likely given the impact of natural disasters and the economic crisis.

The 20 percent devaluation of the currency is likely to help narrow Fiji's current account deficit to 21 percent of GDP in 2009 from 26 percent in 2008 despite a 15 percent drop in tourist arrivals and reduced exports of garments and mineral water. Further improvements in the deficit may be constrained, however, should global demand for Fiji's exports remain weak, and domestic factors limit the supply of sugar and garments for export. In the first half of 2009, remittances were little changed in U.S. dollar terms from a year earlier, but were up 18 percent in local currency terms, helping support domestic consumption. Fiji's foreign exchange reserves declined to a low of $336 million in February 2009 (equivalent to 2.7 months of imports) before recovering to US$500 million in September 2009. Of the increase, $95 million was accounted by the general allocation of SDRs by the IMF in August.

The pass-through of the devaluation of the currency into domestic prices, combined with a recent pickup in oil and food prices due to flood-related shortages, is likely to boost 12-month inflation to 9.5 percent by December 2009. Earlier, the decline in prices for imported food and fuel caused prices to drop year-on-year by June after a 10 percent increase in the twelve months through September 2008.

The Interim Administration's 2009 budget targets the fiscal deficit to widen to 4 percent of GDP in 2009 from 1.5 percent in 2008 because of measures to support domestic demand. The 2009 budget planned higher capital expenditure to be financed in part by a hike in import duties (from 27 percent to 32 percent on average), and improved revenue compliance and collection. After the floods and as the global crisis took its toll, however, tax receipts fell below budget targets. Government expenditure for the first half of 2009 was also lower than budgeted amid lagging execution of capital expenditures.

Looking ahead, Fiji's economy faces several challenges. Firstly, there are substantial downside risks should the global recovery sputter and prices for imported oil continue to increase. Secondly, the devaluation of the currency will likely increase the cost of servicing external debt and add further strains to the budget. Thirdly, Fiji relations with key external partners remain strained and restoration of full bilateral relations remains dependent on Fiji's return to democracy.

Foreign exchange reserves

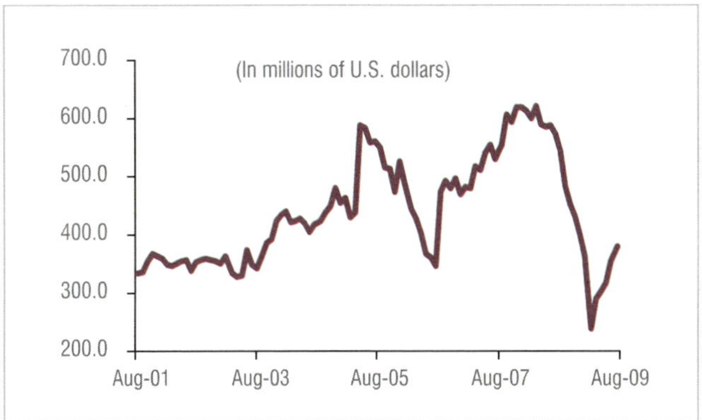

Fiji: Key Indicators

	2004	2005	2006	2007	2008	2009e	2010f
Output, Employment and Prices							
GDP (% change y-y)	5.5	0.6	3.4	-6.6	0.2	-0.3	1.8
Tourist arrivals (thousands)	503	550	545	540	585	550	..
(% change y-y)	16.7	9.4	-0.9	-1.0	8.4	-6.0	..
Unemployment rate (%)	..	..	..	..	..	..	..
Consumer price index (% change y-y)	2.8	2.4	2.5	4.3	6.6	9.5	2.0
Public Sector							
Government balance (% GDP)	-3.1	-3.4	-2.8	-1.7	-1.5	-3.0	-2.0
Domestic public sector debt (% GDP)	44.7	44.5	44.6	43.0	40.5	40.6	38.7
Foreign Trade, BOP and External Debt							
Trade balance (millions US$)	-620	-764	-929	-875	-1,295	-946	..
Exports of goods (millions US$)	666	698	711	754	923	654	..
(% change y-y)	3.9	4.8	1.9	6.0	22.4	-29.1	..
Key export (% change y-y) 1/	1.4	9.6	-6.1	-7.2	34.0	-29.0	..
Imports of goods (millions US$)	1,286	1,462	1,640	1,629	2,218	1,601	..
(% change y-y)	20.8	13.7	12.2	-0.7	36.1	-27.8	..
Current account balance millions US$)	-370	-396	-715	-583	-790	-833	..
(% GDP)	-13.6	-13.2	-22.8	-17.3	-22.0	-23.8	..
Foreign direct investment (millions US$)	103	-15	373	283	292	279	..
Total external debt (millions US$)	357	396	556	462	..	..	..
(% GDP)	13.1	13.2	17.7	13.1	..	..	..
Short-term debt (millions US$)	75	111	111	210	210	..	..
Debt service (% exports of g&s)	1.5	1.3	1.7	1.9	2.7	..	..
Foreign exchange reserves (millions US$) 2/	636	471	520	619	431	..	..
(months of imports g&s)	5.6	4.0	3.7	4.4	2.9	..	..
Financial Markets							
Domestic credit (% change y-y) 3/	18.0	24.5	23.7	6.9	6.4	..	..
Short-term interest rate % p.a.)	1.8	2.3	..	4.3	..	..	..
Exchange rate (FJ$/US$, eop)	1.6	1.7	1.7	1.5	1.8	2.1	..
Real effective exchange rate (2000=100)	109.8	109.2	107.0	109.8	117.7	..	..
(% change y-y)	2.0	-0.5	-2.1	2.6	7.2	..	..
Memo: Nominal GDP (millions US$)	2,727	2,963	3,167	3,375	3,589	3,498	..

e = estimate
f = forecast
1/ Sugar.
2/ Includes foreign assets of non-bank financial institutions.
3/ Domestic credit to the private sector.

INDONESIA

Population	226 million
Population growth	1.2 percent
Surface area	1,905,000 sq. km.
Capital	Jakarta

In the first half of 2009, Indonesia's economy recovered solidly from the relatively weak second half of 2008. Seasonally adjusted real GDP growth has quickened since the start of 2009, with the trend of gradual recovery expected to continue through 2011.

Indonesia's recovery has been supported by an improved external environment. Second-quarter growth rates across the country's major export partners were better than expected, with most trading partners exited recession by mid-year. International prices of many of Indonesia's exports have also recovered in part since their drop from the 2008 peaks. These developments have supported Indonesia's economy, with exports recovering faster than imports.

Domestic consumption continued to contribute strongly to growth in the second quarter. In the first quarter, large amounts of spending by campaign teams for the parliamentary election lifted private consumption. Higher government consumption has been a key driver of growth in the second quarter, by contrast, as the government accelerated disbursement of its 2009 budget. Ongoing resilience in domestic consumption has supported the services sector, with output accelerating compared with Q1. Most other indicators of domestic economic conditions have also strengthened from the start of the year, with consumer confidence at historical highs and rising, retail and vehicle sales improving, and industrial activity recovering from its downturn in late 2008.

Despite this resilience in the overall economy and the improving business environment, investors have remained cautious into the second half of 2009. Purchases of capital equipment continue to be cut, although investment growth in new buildings has remained buoyant. The slowdown in overall investment coincides with flat lending to firms for investment and working capital from late 2008, in contrast to the rapid lending growth in early 2008.

Indonesia's banking sector has remained in good health overall. Non-performing loan ratios are stable, contrary to concerns at the beginning of 2009 that they would rise as borrowers affected by the weaker economy would be unable to meet their commitments. In September 2009, the central bank left its policy interest rate unchanged, following an easing of 300 basis points over the previous 9 months. Only a limited proportion of the cuts in the policy rate have been passed onto the lending rates of commercial banks, however, leading the central bank in late August to ask the 14 largest banks in the country to progressively lower their savings deposit rates to no more than 150 bps above the key policy rate. The central bank hopes that this will reduce the cost of funds for banks, allowing them to lend more and at lower interest rates.

Indonesia's financial markets have continued to strengthen, generally by more than markets elsewhere in the region. The rupiah has appreciated against the weakening U.S. dollar to about 9,000per U.S. dollar by October. The equity market has also performed strongly, rising by one-third from late May to October. By mid-June, yields on government rupiah-denominated bonds had returned to their levels of early 2008. These improved market conditions have allowed the government to continue financing its budget through the domestic bond market, in addition to the two issues of dollar-denominated bonds, accessing funds at longer maturities and at lower yields.

Improved financial market conditions have coincided with somewhat less volatile flows on Indonesia's capital accounts, rendering Indonesia's external position in September 2009 more robust than at the start of the year. The overall balance of payments remained in surplus in the second quarter, although by less than in the first one. The current account surplus increased slightly, as the improved external environment lifted exports more than imports. While non-resident investors returned as net purchasers of Indonesian financial assets, overall the capital account switched to deficit, largely due to slower net foreign direct investment following several quarters of record inflows. Indonesia's scheduled external debt was largely rolled over through the first half of 2009, countering concerns early in the year that roll-over rates may be low and that the amount of debt due may be greater than officially reported. Foreign reserves had recovered to $62 billion, near the peak of mid-2008.

After remaining subdued for longer than expected, inflation started to pick up from July and August. Twelve-month headline inflation amounted to 2.8 percent, while core inflation excluding prices for food and energy was 4.8 percent. All in all, Indonesia's inflation fell faster than in most of its trading partners, but remains higher than in almost all of them.

Indonesia: Key Indicators

	2006	2007	2008	2009e	2010f	2008		2009		2009			
	Year	Year	Year	Year	Year	Q3	Q4	Q1	Q2	Jun	Jul	Aug	Sep
Output, Employment and Prices													
Real GDP (% change y-y) 1/	5.5	6.3	6.1	4.3	5.4	6.4	5.2	4.4	4.0	..	..	..	..
Industrial production index (2000=100)	110	124	128	..	..	130	124	125	128	129	..	..	..
(% change y-y)	-1.6	12.6	3.3	..	..	-0.8	-2.8	0.2	0.7	1.0	..	..	..
Unemployment (%)	10.3	9.1	9.4	..	..	..	..	..	..	..	..	..	..
Real wages (% change y-y)	3.5	1.3	..	..	..	..	..	..	..	..	..	..	..
Consumer price index (% change y-y)	13.1	6.4	11.1	4.7	5.6	12.0	11.5	3.7	2.8	3.7	2.7	2.8	2.8
Public Sector													
Government balance (% GDP)	-0.9	-1.3	-0.1	-2.2	-0.7	..	..	..	..	..	..	..	..
Domestic public sector debt (% GDP)	39.2	34.3	29.1	28	24	..	..	..	..	..	..	..	..
Foreign Trade, BOP and External Debt													
Trade balance (billions US$)	23.8	25.9	14.0	16.9	11.9	3.2	4.6	7.0	8.7	1.4	1.0	1.2	..
Exports of goods (billions US$)	103.5	118.0	139.3	123.4	136.2	38.1	29.8	24.2	27.5	9.4	9.7	10.5	..
(% change y-y)	19.0	14.0	18.0	-11.4	10.4	26.9	-7.5	-29.7	-26.3	-26.8	-22.7	-15.4	..
Key export (% change y-y) 2/	10.3	4.1	31	..	..	39.0	-48.7	-53.8	-51.9	..	..	..	..
Imports of goods (billions US$)	79.8	85.3	116.7	95.0	107.9	34.9	25.6	17.2	18.8	7.9	8.7	9.3	..
(% change y-y)	6.3	15.4	36.9	-18.6	13.6	43.5	12.6	-35.9	-41.1	-34.5	-32.5	-24.6	..
Current account balance (billions US$)	10.9	10.5	0.6	9.0	2.0	-0.9	-0.7	2.9	3.1	..	..	..	..
(% GDP)	3.0	2.4	0.1	1.7	0.4	-0.7	-0.2	2.6	2.4	..	..	..	..
Foreign direct investment (billions US$) 3/	4.9	6.9	8.3	..	..	1.9	3.3	2.5	1.0	..	..	..	..
External debt (billions US$)	123.7	137.3	149.9	..	..	148.1	149.9	148.6	150.2	..	..	..	..
(% GDP)	33.4	33.2	31.9	..	..	..	..	..	..	..	..	..	..
Foreign exchange reserves (billions US$)	41.1	55.0	51.6	42.5	..	57.1	51.6	54.8	57.6	57.6	57.4	57.9	62.3
(months of imports of g&s)	5.6	6.5	4.5	..	..	4.4	3.9	4.2	4.4	..	..	..	..
Financial Markets													
Domestic credit (% change y-y)	8.5	15.3	13	..	..	16.8	13.5	16.6	14.1	14.6	17.7	13.4	..
Short-term interest rate (% p.a.) 4/	8.4	5.2	8.6	..	..	9.2	9.7			..	..	..	..
Exchange rate (Rupiah/US$, ave)	9134	9162	9802	10516	10000	9252	11510	11575	10225	10225	9920	10060	9681
Real effective exchange rate (2000=100)	133.8	134.3	129.5	..	..	138.0	119.9	117.7	129.7	129.7	..	..	..
(% change y-y)	17.1	0.4	-3.6	..	..	3.3	-6.9	-8.4	-2.8	-2.8	..	..	..
Stock market index (Aug. 1988=100) 5/	1806	2746	1355	..	..	1833	1355	1434	2027	2027	2323	2342	2468
Memo: Nominal GDP (billions US$)	364	431	463	450	..	144	115	111	131	..	..	..	..

Source: National data sources.
f = forecast
1/ Based on GDP 2000 base
2/ Crude oil exports
3/ Uses new classification starting in 1994
4/ Policy rate: one-month Bank Indonesia Certificates
5/ Jakarta Composite

Employment grew faster than the working age population in the year to February, helping reduce the unemployment rate. However, most new jobs are in the informal sector, especially for women. Higher employment, low inflation and the final tranches of the government's unconditional cash transfer program (BLT), have helped reduce the poverty rate to 14.2 percent by March 2009, or by 1.2 percentage points from a year earlier.

Public finances have provided a larger stimulus to the economy in 2009 than in recent years. Through July, the government budget overall was in larger deficit than in previous years, thanks to lower revenues due to tax cuts under the fiscal stimulus package and weaker profits as a result of lower commodity prices and weaker external demand. Government spending on its core programs was broadly unchanged in nominal terms compared with 2008, but lower subsidies for energy resulted in lower overall outlays. After a very slow start, disbursement of the spending measures under the government's stimulus package accelerated from mid-July. For the year as a whole, the fiscal deficit is likely to widen to about 2.2 percent of GDP, somewhat less than under the 2009 budget. For 2010, the draft budget targets a deficit of 1.6 percent of GDP. The government's conservative nominal GDP growth and oil price assumptions, however, suggest that there may be room for larger spending than budgeted within the overall deficit projection.

Economic recovery is likely to continue. Real GDP growth is expected to rise gradually further towards its potential of a little over 6 percent by 2011. Domestic demand is likely to remain the main driver of growth, helped by the fiscal stimulus this year and by the recovery in investor confidence in 2010. Net exports should not subtract greatly from growth once global recovery is on a firmer recovery path, perhaps by 2011. With a weakening trade surplus and recovery in commodity prices, the current account is likely to move closer to balance or even to a small deficit by 2011.

LAO PDR

Population	5.9 million
Population growth	1.7 percent
Surface area	237,000 sq.km.
Capital	Vientiane

The economy of Lao PDR has performed relatively well in the midst of the global financial crisis. Real GDP is projected to grow at 6.4 percent in 2009, slightly lower than the 7.3 percent in 2008. This projection has been revised upwards from 5 percent earlier in the year because most sectors, including mining, manufacturing (garment, food and beverages, cement and metal industries), construction, agriculture and services have been performing better than expected due to the recent recovery of commodity prices (copper and gold), increased public expenditures and recovery in regional demand (especially from China). The mining sector (mostly copper and gold) contributes about 2.5 percentage points to growth this year; manufacturing and construction together, and agriculture about 1 percentage points, and services account for the remainder.

With the expected global recovery, real GDP growth in Lao PDR will strengthen over the medium-term although the recovery remains subject to global commodity price changes (mainly metals and agriculture). The economy is projected to benefit from the recovery of tourism, implementation of large hydropower projects under construction and in the pipeline and projected increase in demand from the neighboring countries (especially Thailand, China and Vietnam); and to the European Union.

Prices have been falling year-on-year since May, reaching a drop of 2.3 percent by August due to the decline in food and energy prices. Core inflation excluding food and energy fell to 0.9 percent year-on-year in August. Average inflation is projected to decline from 7.6 percent in 2008 to just about 1 percent this year, but should increase slowly over the medium term as prices for oil and food recover.

Pressure from the global crisis combined with commitments to host a series of major events led to significant expansion of public outlays in 2009. As a result, the budget deficit is estimated to increase sharply from 1.8 percent in 2008 to 6.8 percent in 2009. Public spending has noticeably increased on capital expenditure and the wage bill (the increase in public servants wages and allowances was approved by parliament before the crisis). There was an increase in quasi-fiscal expenditure, as the central bank lent in support of local infrastructure projects and preparation for two important events, the South-East Asian (SEA) Games and the 450 year Vientiane Anniversary. After three years of exceeding budget targets, revenues are expected to fall short of target this year by about 8 percent. While Lao PDR has made progress in reducing its external and public debt burden, it still faces a high risk of debt. Nevertheless, public debt service remains manageable as much of the debt is contracted on concessional terms.

In dollar terms, Lao PDR's exports and imports are expected to fall this year due to lower commodity prices, smaller imports for large infrastructure projects and weaker global demand. Exports are projected to drop by about 10 percent while imports would decline slightly more by 11 percent. The current account deficit is projected to narrow to about 8 percent in 2009, with foreign exchange reserves down to $586 million or about 4.9 months of non-resource imports.

Real GDP growth and fiscal balance

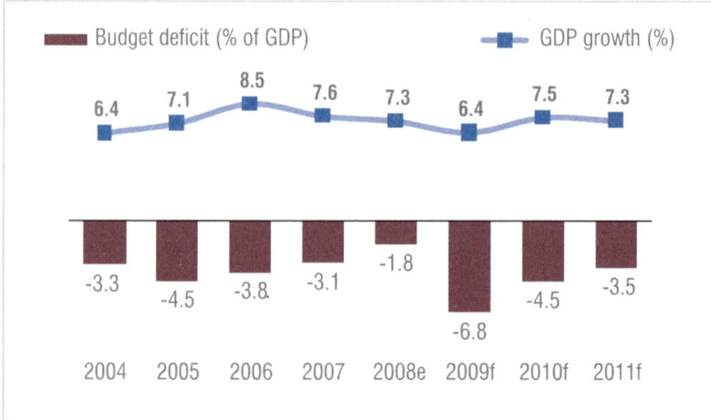

The kip has remained little changed against the U.S. dollar during the first eight months of 2009 and risen modestly by 2.4 percent against the Thai baht. This followed a larger appreciation in 2008.

Credit has continued to grow rapidly, with 12-month credit growth up to 98 percent by the end of June from 78 percent in December 2008. The sharp increase in lending against the background of poor capacity to screen borrowers raises concerns about an increase in contingent liabilities and possible deterioration of bank balance sheets. This fast expansion takes place however from a very low base, with credit amounting to 12 percent of GDP at the end of 2008.

Reforms have shown some progress. Most importantly, the government has committed to returning to a more sustainable macroeconomic path and a phasing out of quasi-fiscal activities. Public finance management reforms include completing the provincial level centralization of the Treasury, Customs and Tax this year and the full extent by next year. Consolidation of revenue accounts with the National Treasury is also in progress, as is the revision and implementation of various laws and decrees, including the VAT law, the tax law, the executive decrees on minerals and royalties, and on the civil service administration. The government is also moving ahead with the elimination of the tax exemption on motor vehicle imports. A new decree on new import and export licensing procedures has also been approved, as have been the mineral law and the new unified law on investment promotion.

Lao PDR: Key Indicators

	2004	2005	2006	2007	2008	2009e	2010f
Output, Employment and Prices							
Real GDP (% change y-y)	6.4	7.1	8.5	7.6	7.3	6.4	7.5
Consumer price index (% change y-y)	10.5	7.2	6.8	4.5	7.6	1.0	3.5
Public Sector 1/							
Government balance (% GDP) 2/	-3.3	-4.5	-3.8	-3.1	-1.8	-6.8	-4.5
Foreign Trade, BOP and External Debt							
Trade balance (millions US$)	-520	-534	-426	-736	-915	-772	-684.3
Exports of goods (millions US$)	536	725	1,080	1,188	1,422	1,304	1527.5
(% change y-y)	19.1	35.2	49.0	10.0	19.7	-8.3	17.1
Key export (% change y-y)	10.8	33.0	49.2	6.1	19.4	-8.5	19.0
Imports of goods (millions US$)	1,056	1,258	1,506	1,924	2,337	2,076	2211.9
(% change y-y)	52.2	19.2	19.6	27.8	21.5	-11.1	6.5
Current account balance (millions US$)	-413	-453	-350	-532	-706	-468	-391.1
(% GDP)	-17.1	-16.6	-9.9	-12.4	-12.7	-7.9	-5.9
Foreign direct investment (millions US$)	315	335	625	617	771	614	561.1
External debt (millions US$)	2,648	3,088	3,424	4,301	5,145	5,548	5796.9
(% GDP)	105.6	113.2	97.2	100.3	92.8	93.3	88.2
Short-term debt (millions US$)	95	109	..	..	..	..	...
Debt service (% exports of g&s)	17.4	20.9	5.7	12.5	10.3	265.7	270.7
Foreign exchange reserves (millions US$) 3/	226	238	335	539	636	587	675.4
(months of imports of g&s)	3.8	3.0	3.1	4.3	4.2	4.0	4.0
Financial Markets							
Domestic credit (% change y-y)	9.7	5.5	-6.0	16.0	84.6	45.0	30.0
Short-term interest rate (% p.a.) 4/	16.0	15.0	14.5	13.0	13.0	12.5	12.0
Exchange rate (Kip/US$, ave)	10581.9	10635.8	10060.6	9562.9	8994.1	8505.8	8548.3
Exchange rate (Kip/US$, eop)	10357.0	10676.0	9655.0	9341.0	8466.0	8527.0	8569.7
Real effective exchange rate (2000=100)	95.9	103.1	105.5	104.3	123.5	..	..
(% change y-y)	-1.7	7.5	2.3	-1.1	18.4	..	..
Memo: Nominal GDP (millions US$)	2,419	2,728	3,522	4,287	5,544	5,947	6,570.1

Source: National data sources.
f = forecast
1/ Fiscal year basis
2/ After grants
3/ Excluding gold
4/ Treasury bill rate

MALAYSIA

Population	27 million
Population growth	1.7 percent
Surface area	330,000 sq.km.
Capital	Kuala Lumpur

After a period of strong growth, Malaysia's economy has been hit hard by the global economic downturn. The deterioration in economic conditions first became apparent in the manufacturing sector towards the end of 2008, when both private investment and exports contracted sharply. Real GDP growth slowed to 4.8 percent in 2008, as a result, from 5.8 percent on average in the previous three years. In early 2009, the manufacturing-led downturn intensified and spread more widely through the economy, from the tradable into the non-tradable sector and from corporate into household demand. This resulted in a sizeable drop in output during the first two quarters of 2009, with manufacturing down 13 percent from a year earlier.

Economic activity showed signs of improvement in the second quarter of 2009. In seasonally adjusted terms, consumption, fixed investment, and exports all expanded in the second quarter. The services sector also improved. Conditions in the electrical and electronics (E&E) industry, which accounted for an important part of the contraction, improved in line with these general developments. Aggregate capital utilization increased as well, and so did consumer and business confidence.

Malaysia's export performance tells an important part of the story. Exports fell by some 31 percent year-on-year during January-July. Since April, exports have grown at an average monthly rate of 4 percent (seasonally adjusted) on the back of stronger demand from the U.S. and several countries in East Asia. Shipments to the EU and Japan remain weak, however, highlighting the fragile nature of the recovery. Good sequential growth was observed in exports of E&E goods, chemical products, and palm oil, even though on a yearly basis levels are still much below last year's.

Other external indicators improved as well. Malaysia's financial account of the balance of payments registered a deficit of $38.3 billion in the second half of 2008 compared to a surplus of $4.8 billion in the first half because of a sharp decline of foreign direct investment (FDI) and the large net outflows of portfolio and other private investment, as investors rushed to boost liquidity in their home markets. Portfolio outflows moderated this year, helping reduce the deficit on the financial account to $15 billion in the first half of 2009. The current account surplus meanwhile stabilized at about 18 percent of GDP. Foreign exchange reserves fell from $126 billion in the middle of 2008 to $94 billion in September 2009, but are still four times larger than short-term external debt.

Corporate sector and labor market indicators suggest a mixed picture. On the positive side, the number of newly registered companies rebounded in recent months after a sharp slowdown between August 2008 and February 2009. The current level (around 4,000 new firms per month) is now similar to that of July last year. But the number of bankruptcies is still rising. The July-August average (1,420 firms per month) is 13 percent higher than the average in the first half of the year. Job retrenchments were recorded at 12,590 positions in the first quarter of 2009 compared to 13,851 for 2008 as a whole, with actual job losses likely to have been much higher. The unemployment rate rose to 4 percent by March, the highest since mid-2003. The labor market has stabilized somewhat thereafter, with employment both in the manufacturing and service sector on the rise.

Real GDP growth: the power of inventories

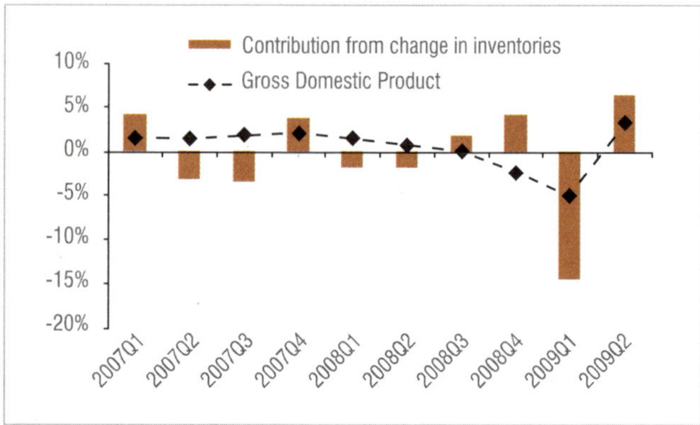

The banking sector remained in good health, thanks to conservative prudential standards, adequate capitalization, and limited linkages to toxic securities and troubled financial institutions in industrial economies. The capital adequacy ratio of the banking system averaged at a comfortable 14.6 percent as of August and nonperforming loans amounted to 2.1 percent of total loans, with credit risks being concentrated in the manufacturing sector.

Overall poverty remained unchanged in 2008, but rural poverty worsened. Despite a sharp economic slowdown in the final quarter, Malaysia's poverty incidence last year remained

Malaysia: Key Indicators

	2006	2007	2008	2009e	2010f	2008		2009		2009			
	Year	Year	Year	Year	Year	Q3	Q4	Q1	Q2	Jun	Jul	Aug	Sep
Output, Employment and Prices													
Real GDP (% change y-y)	5.8	6.3	4.6	-2.3	4.1	4.8	0.1	-6.2	-3.9	..	..	..	..
Industrial production index (2000=100)	104.8	107.2	107.8	..	..	110.3	101.1	94.6	97.3	97.9	105.1	104	..
(% change y-y)	4.8	2.3	0.6	..	..	1.0	-8.3	-6.5	2.8	-9.5	-8.2	-5.7	..
Unemployment (%)	3.3	3.2	3.3	..	..	3.1	3.1	4.0	3.6	..	..	..	..
Real wages (% change y-y)	..	..	..	..	..	..	..	..	..	..	..	..	..
Consumer price index (% change y-y)	3.6	2.0	5.4	-0.1	1.5	8.4	5.9	3.7	1.3	-1.4	-2.4	-2.4	..
Public Sector													
Government balance (% GDP) /1	-3.3	-3.2	-4.8	-7.8	-6.4	-3.9	-10.3	-4.3	-7.5	..	..	..	..
Domestic public sector debt (% GDP) 1/	37.9	38.5	39.6	..	..	36.4	43.3	51.0	52.0	..	..	..	..
Foreign Trade, BOP and External Debt													
Trade balance (billions US$)	29.5	29.2	45.3	..	..	12.4	11.7	9.2	7.5	2.6	2.2	2.7	..
Exports of goods (billions US$)	160.6	176.0	209.7	..	..	55.5	52.0	33.5	36.4	12.8	13.8	13.6	..
(% change y-y)	14.0	9.6	19.1	..	..	21.8	6.7	-28.8	-33.2	-28.4	-29.3	-23.0	..
Key export (% change y-y) 2/	6.4	-4.2	-3.8	..	..	2.6	-17.2	-19.1	-22.8	-16.3	-15.2	-13.1	..
Imports of goods (billions US$)	131.1	146.8	164.4	..	..	43.1	40.3	24.3	28.9	10.2	11.6	10.9	..
(% change y-y)	14.6	12.0	12.0	..	..	15.0	0.4	-37.2	-30.9	-26.7	-23.1	-17.9	..
Current account balance (billions US$)	25.5	29.2	38.8	..	..	11.5	8.4	8.6	8.1	..	..	..	..
(% GDP)	16.3	15.7	17.5	..	..	19.5	16.7	20.2	17.8	..	..	..	..
Foreign direct investment (billions US$)	6.1	8.5	7.2	..	..	0.3	4.1	2.8	0.9	..	..	..	..
External debt (billions US$)	50.9	55.8	66.4	..	..	75.3	66.4	68.3	65.7	..	..	..	..
(% GDP)	32.5	29.9	29.9	..	..	32.9	32.5	40.1	35.9	..	..	..	..
Short-term debt (billions US$)	11.8	16.2	22.4	..	..	30.6	22.4	24.3	24.3	..	..	..	..
Debt service (% exports of g&s)	7.3	2.6	3.1	..	..	2.2	3.1	7.8	8.1	..	..	..	..
Foreign exchange reserves (billions US$)	82.2	101.5	91.6	..	..	109.7	91.6	87.9	91.7	91.7	91.3	93.3	96.2
(months of imports of g&s) 3/	7.8	8.4	7.4	..	..	8.9	7.6	8.3	9.0	9.0	7.9	8.5596	..
Financial Markets													
Domestic credit (% change y-y)	6.3	8.6	12.8	..	..	10.5	11.3	11.2	9.3	8.3	8.4	..	..
Short-term interest rate (% p.a.) 4/	3.5	3.5	3.5	..		3.6	3.5	2.5	2.1	2.1	2.1	2.1	..
Exchange rate (Ringgit/US$, eop)	3.53	3.31	3.46	..	..	3.46	3.46	3.65	3.52	3.52	3.52	3.53	3.48
Real effective exchange rate (2000=100) 5/	99.2	102.6	103.3	..	..	104.6	101.4	100.5	100.8	100.0	..	..	..
(% change y-y)	4.0	3.4	0.7	..	..	0.9	-2.4	-3.9	-0.6	-1.1	..	..	..
Stock market index (Apr. 4, 1986=100) 6/	1096	1445	877	..	..	1019	877	873	1075	1075	1175	1174	1202
Memo: Nominal GDP (billions US$)	156.4	186.7	222.2	..	..	57.2	51.1	42.6	45.8	..	..	..	..

Sources: National data sources, World Bank staff estimates.
f = forecast
1/ Federal government only.
2/ Electronics.
3/ Excludes services imports.
4/ One-month interbank rate.
5/ World Bank's staff estimate.
6/ KLSE Composite.

unchanged from 2007 at 3.6 percent of all households. Contrary to expectations, urban poverty decreased slightly, as lower manufacturing employment in late-2008 did not have an immediate poverty impact. Rural poverty, however, rose to 7.4 percent from 7.1 percent. In 2009, an overall increase in poverty is possible given the decline in economic growth for the year as a whole.

The near-term outlook argues for a slow process of recovery. Real GDP is projected to contract 2.3 percent in 2009 before increasing 4.1 percent in 2010. Consumption and fixed investment growth will remain relatively subdued, due to uncertainties about the global outlook, the efforts of fiscal consolidation, and still-low levels of capacity utilization. The turnaround in the inventory cycle is expected to be a main driver of growth. Import growth should continue to outpace export growth in the coming quarters, resulting in a smaller trade surplus. The current account balance is expected to decline to 12.3 percent of GDP in 2009 and further to 12.1 percent in 2010.

Fiscal and monetary policies helped contain the negative impact of the crisis on domestic demand. The fiscal packages announced in November 2008 and March 2009 (SP1 and SP2), amounted to RM7 billion (1 percent of GDP) and RM60 billion (9 percent). Under the SP2, the actual fiscal injection amount to RM15 billion to be spent in 2009 and 2010, with the rest accounted for measures without a direct fiscal impact. Despite higher revenues, government expenditures expanded much faster in the first half of 2009, leading to the largest first-half deficit in decades. The deficit is likely to widen from 4.8 percent of GDP in 2008 to 7.8 percent in 2009. Fiscal consolidation efforts have been announced recently and should help narrow the deficit to 6.4 percent of GDP in 2010. Monetary policy has been accommodative after a 150 basis point reduction in the overnight policy in three steps to 2 percent and the required reserve ratio by 300 basis points to 1 percent during late-2008 and early-2009. Both rates currently stand at historically low levels.

The crisis has not detracted attention from the underlying weaknesses which the authorities are addressing under the umbrella of a new economic model. Malaysia's economy has been trapped at upper-middle income levels for some time now. The authorities aim to revitalize growth with an integrated strategy focused on the specialization of the economy into new niches and the upgrading of the skill base of its workforce. Efforts in formulating a new economic model are under way and will build further on the important steps that have been already introduced to improve the dynamism of the service sector.

MONGOLIA

Population	2.6 million
Population growth	0.9 percent
Surface area	1,567,000 sq.km.
Capital	Ulan Batar

Mongolia has been one of the countries in East Asia hardest hit by the financial crisis, although unlike others, the crisis was transmitted via the commodity channel. The collapse in copper prices that began in July 2008 hit Mongolia harder than the other major copper producers (Chile, Peru, Papua New Guinea and Zambia), because of the country's particular combination of expansive fiscal and monetary policies, a fixed exchange rate and – at that time - an overheating financial sector.

The government took strong actions to address the economic downturn from the start of 2009, supported by programs with the IMF, the World Bank, the ADB and Japan. These have led to a stabilization of the external sector, the exchange rate and the budget. The trade balance has improved, but this is in part caused by the sharper contraction in imports than exports due to the economic downturn itself. Attention now is shifting to tackling the strains in the financial sector and ameliorating the effects of the downturn on the real economy, unemployment, and poverty.

The latest developments show that the budget remains under pressure, as revenues have continue to drop, whereas expenditures remain little changed. During the boom years of 2003-07, the government ran modest fiscal surpluses, but these turned out to be insufficient to absorb the fiscal shock caused by the collapse of the mineral prices and spending plans based on these prices remaining high. Moreover, the fiscal shock was made worse by government policies during the boom years to shift the fiscal burden away from the non-mining sector, leaving the budget increasingly dependent on revenues from mining.

The global downturn also aggravated problems in the financial sector which had been overheating during the boom years. During the boom, very high inflation (33.7 percent year-on-year in August 2008, the highest in East Asia) and loose monetary policies led to a credit boom that masked growth in non-performing loans (NPLs). High inflation also led to negative real interest rates on local currency deposits, resulting in flight of local currency savings into foreign exchange deposits, where interest rates were as high as 12-18 percent in some banks. As a result the successful policy actions by the central bank – including interest rate hikes and auctioning of foreign exchange - deposits have now recovered. However, non-performing loans have continued to increase, and bank lending to the private sector has come to a virtual standstill, as banks prefer to invest in central bank bills instead.

For 2009, Mongolia is facing a major slowdown in real GDP growth to an estimated 0.5 percent from 8.9 percent in 2008. Unemployment has been steadily increasing since the beginning of the year as a result of the contraction in the real sector. A recent survey of the informal urban sector and a recently commissioned study on the crisis implications for household in the informal sector found that the effects of the economic slowdown have a widespread social and poverty impact in Mongolia. Real effective income has fallen by about 60 percent in some informal urban labor markets, due to high inflation eroding real wages and due to reduced job availability. Employment conditions are also becoming less favorable for informal workers in the rural regions, and herders and informal mining workers are barely able to cope with the decreasing job availability, falling wages and increasing living expenses.

Nonperforming loans and loans in arrears

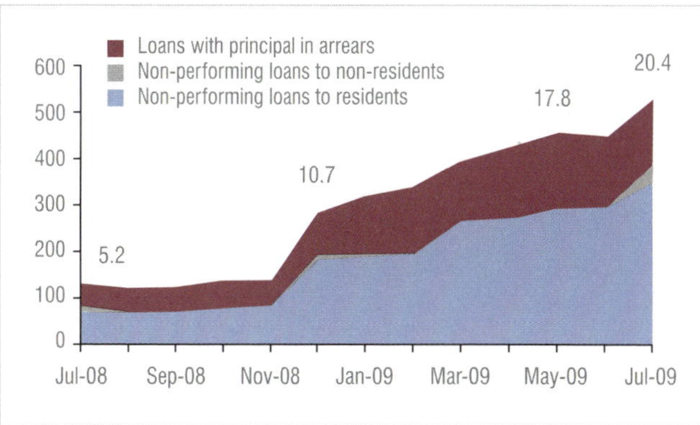

Recently, Parliament voted to approve four draft law amendments necessary for the conclusion of the Oyu Tolgoi (OT) investment agreement between the government and Ivanhoe Mines/Rio Tinto. If the deal is concluded, the Oyu Tolgoi copper and gold mine will make a substantial contribution to the economic growth of Mongolia in the near future.

Going forward, it is important that the government focuses on implementing a fiscal responsibility framework to avoid a repeat of the boom-and-bust spending pattern that Mongolia has just experienced. It is also important to improve the planning and budgeting for public investments, and to prioritize the protection of infrastructure maintenance—critical during the downturn. Protecting the poor during this downturn is a challenge, but can be achieved by starting to target the currently untargeted social grants (in particular, the Child Money Program). In the financial sector, the authorities should ensure stability by intensifying supervision and taking decisive action in case of bank failures in order to retain confidence in the financial sector. In addition, a restructuring of the banking sector is envisaged after the completion of a series of loan portfolio audits. In the mining sector, the government can now use the recent experience gained during the negotiations of the OT investment agreement to improve the overall policy environment.

Mongolia: Key Indicators

	2004	2005	2006	2007	2008	2009e	2010f
Output, Employment and Prices							
Real GDP (% change y-y)	10.6	7.3	8.6	10.2	8.9	0.5	3.0
Industrial production index	..	..	100.0	110.4	113.4	..	..
(% change y-y)	..	..	..	10.4	2.8	..	..
Unemployment (%)	3.6	3.3	3.2	2.8	2.8	..	..
Consumer price index (% change y-y)	10.9	9.6	5.9	14.1	23.2	8.5	..
Public Sector							
Government balance (% GDP)	-1.8	2.6	8.1	2.8	-5.0	-6.5	..
Domestic public sector debt (% GDP)	1.4	0.1	1.0	0.5	0.0	0.0	..
Foreign Trade, BOP and External Debt							
Trade balance (millions US$)	-99	-100	136	-52	613	-183	..
Exports of goods (millions US$)	872	1,066	1,544	1,951	2,535	1,830	..
(% change y-y)	39.0	22.2	44.8	26.4	29.9	-27.7	..
Key export (% change y-y) 1/	..	14.7	94.8	27.7	3.0	..	..
Imports of goods (millions US$)	971	1,166	1,408	2,003	3,147	2,013	..
(% change y-y)	17.5	20.0	20.8	42.3	57.1	-35.7	..
Current account balance (millions US$)	24	30	222	265	-722	-291	..
(% GDP)	1.3	1.3	7.0	6.7	-13.9	-6.9	..
Foreign direct investment (millions US$)	129	258	290	360	586	517	..
External debt (millions US$)	1,312	1,360	1,414	1,529	1,601	1,860	..
(% GDP)	73.7	59.7	44.3	38.9	33.1	46.5	..
Short-term debt (millions US$) 2/	0.0	0.0	0.0	0.0	0.0	..	..
Debt service (% exports of g&s) 3/	9.4	7.6	5.4	4.3	3.5	4.3	..
Foreign exchange reserves (millions US$)	208	333	718	1,001	657	822	..
(month of imports of g&s)	1.8	2.5	4.6	5.0	2.1	3.7	..
Financial Markets							
Domestic credit (% change y-y)	25.8	18.8	-3.1	78.4	60.6	..	..
Short-term interest rate (% p.a.) 4/	15.8	3.7	5.1	8.4	9.8	..	..
Exchange rate (Tugrik/US$, eop)	1209.0	1221.0	1165.0	1170.0	1267.5	..	..
Real effective exchange rate (2000=100)	95.4	101.8	107.1	109.0	130.2	..	..
(% change y-y)	-1.5	6.7	5.2	1.8	19.5	..	..
Stock market index (2000=100) 5/	121	204	382	2,048	1,182	..	..
Memo: Nominal GDP (millions US$)	1,814	2,307	3,156	3,930	5,258	..	..

Source: National data sources.
e = estimate
f = forecast
1/ Copper concentrate.
2/ Short-term PPG debt.
3/ On PPG debt.
4/ Yield of 14-day bills until 2006 and of 7-day bills for 2007.
5/ Top-20 index, eop, index=100 in Dec-2000.

PAPUA NEW GUINEA

Population	6.3 million
Population growth	2.0 percent
Surface area	463,000 sq.km.
Capital	Port Moresby

PNG's economy is weathering well the impact of the global economic crisis. In 2009, real GDP growth is projected to slow only moderately to 4-5 percent from an average of 6.5 percent during 2007-08. This extends to 7 years the longest uninterrupted period of economic growth since PNG's independence in 1975. Growth remains broad-based, extending to both the extractive industry and the non-mining sectors, in particular construction and telecommunications. Some sectors such as construction appear to be operating at nearly full capacity. Although the share of formal sector employment in total employment is modest, it is growing rapidly.

Prudent macroeconomic management during the 2005 2008 commodity boom helped PNG build large buffers to cope with the global economic crisis. During the years preceding the crisis, the government prudently capped growth of government spending, saved windfall mineral revenues and paid off more expensive external debt. The non-mineral budget deficit, a key indicator of the fiscal stance in a resource rich economy, remained largely steady around 5-6 percent of GDP, close to the estimated long-term sustainable level. The overall budget was in a large surplus that peaked at 10 percent of GDP in 2007.

Care needs to be taken, however, in calibrating the fiscal response to the global economic crisis, given the already robust growth performance of the economy and the volatility of PNG's future mineral revenue stream. It is understood that one-fourth of the total savings in trust accounts, or 4 percent of GDP, were used to finance government spending in the first half of 2009. Assuming the expenditure trend from the first half continues, the non mineral budget deficit may increase to 10-11 percent of GDP in 2009. Additional fiscal pressures may emerge over the medium term, including from government external borrowing to finance its stake in the PNG Liquefied Natural Gas (LNG) Project (see below) and meet substantial public investment commitments to landowners in conjunction with the project.

The prospect of a major extractive industry project – the PNG LNG Project - is also helping buoy PNG's economy. The project will be implemented by a consortium of international and domestic investors led by Exxon Mobil at an estimated cost of about $17 billion, including finance charges, or more than twice PNG's annual GDP. The project is currently at the front-end engineering and design stage with the final investment decision expected by the end of 2009 and, assuming a positive decision, the start of production around 2014. The confidence boost to the private sector and consumer sentiment from the project combined with the inflow of substantial investment for design and early works have helped limit to an extent the negative impact of the global crisis on the PNG's economy.

The authorities responded well to the drop in external demand. The collapse of commodity prices in mid-2008 and the subsequent capital outflows reduced PNG's foreign exchange reserves from a high of $2.7 billion in mid 2008 to less than US$2 billion by early 2009. Following the tightening of monetary policy in late 2008 early 2009 and the somewhat delayed adjustment of the exchange rate, foreign exchange reserves have been stabilized and recovered to $2.3 billion by September 2009. Tighter monetary policy also helped bring inflation under control after a peak of 13.5 percent year-on-year in the third quarter of 2008.

PNG: Fiscal stance, 2002-09

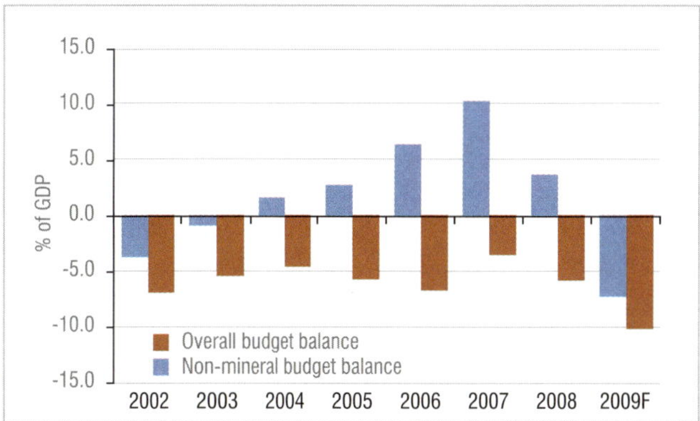

In the medium term, PNG is facing a significant volatility of its export and budget revenue base underscoring the need for continuing prudent fiscal management and expenditure smoothing as implemented in recent years. The PNG LNG project holds a major upside potential in terms of growth and revenues for the PNG economy, both during the construction stage (2010-13) and especially after production starts in 2014. As with other major natural resource projects, however, tax revenues from PNG LNG project are not expected to start flowing until the end of the next decade, several years after the start of production. Meanwhile, in the near term, PNG's revenues from existing extractive projects are projected to start declining. In particular, the Ok Tedi copper mine and South Highlands oil fields, which together currently account for more than a half of merchandise export earnings and government mineral revenue, are expected to come to natural depletion by around 2015.

Translating the strong macroeconomic performance and extractive industry revenues into a broad improvement

Papua New Guinea: Key Indicators

	2004	2005	2006	2007	2008	2009e	2010f
Output, Employment and Prices							
Real GDP (% change y-y)	2.7	3.6	2.6	6.5	6.6	3.9	3.7
Tourist arrivals (thousands)	59.0	69.3	77.7	104.1	115.0	123.0	130.0
(% change y-y)	4.9	17.3	12.2	34.0	10.4	7.0	5.7
Consumer price index (% change y-y)	2.1	1.7	2.3	0.9	10.7	5.3	4.8
Public Sector							
Government balance (% GDP)	1.6	2.7	6.4	10.3	3.7	-1.9	-7.4
Domestic public sector debt (% GDP)	25.2	22.4	18.0	17.0	14.5	14.8	14.3
Foreign Trade, BOP and External Debt							
Trade balance (millions US$)	760	816	1,401	1,419	1,603	676	887
Exports of goods (millions US$)	2,554	3,278	4,207	4,750	5,397	4,197	4,646
(% change y-y)	18.6	28.3	28.3	12.9	13.6	-22.2	10.7
Key export (% change y-y) 1/	10.5	6.0	9.3	25.6	26.3	15.3	6.2
Imports of goods (millions US$)	1,794	2,462	2,805	3,331	3,794	3,521	3,759
(% change y-y)	25.0	37.2	13.9	18.8	13.9	-7.2	6.8
Current account balance (millions US$)	88	207	128	112	228	-546	-393
(% GDP)	2.2	4.2	2.3	1.8	2.8	-6.7	-4.7
Foreign direct investment (millions US$)	25.8	67.9	193.1	462.0	277.1	263.2	276.8
External debt (millions US$)	2,078	2,021	2,175	1,995	2,004	2,225	2,274
(% GDP)	51.8	41.2	38.6	30.7	24.4	27.9	27.1
Short-term debt (millions US$)	109	232	167	100	125	110	107
Debt service (% exports of g&s)	12.5	9.7	8.3	8.4	6.4	7.4	7.3
Foreign exchange reserves (millions US$)	663	765	1,427	2,087	2,093	2,320	2,410
(months of imports of g&s)	2.8	2.4	3.8	4.8	4.3	5.1	5.0
Financial Markets							
Domestic credit (% change y-y)	0.9	23.7	38.2	34.4	41.0	19.6	21.3
Short-term interest rate (% p.a.)	3.1	3.8	3.4	4.4	5.6	7.5	7
Exchange rate (Kina/US$, eop)	3.1	3.1	3.0	2.8	2.7	2.7	2.8
Real effective exchange rate (2000=100)	101.0	108.3	101.8	101.4	116.3	116.3	117.2
(% change y-y)	0.9	7.2	-6.0	-0.4	14.6	0.0	0.8
Memo: Nominal GDP (millions US$)	3,927	4,899	5,605	6,387	8,092	8,200	8,390

Source: National data sources.
e = estimate f = forecast 1/ Gold

in living standards remains a key challenge. Key policies need to include ensuring the integrity of the public financial management and adequate expenditures for sectoral service provision, improving efficiency of sectoral spending, strict control over the size and performance of the civil service, and transparency and accountability in budget management. Thinking also needs to start about setting up more robust institutional structures and mechanisms to save and use the windfalls from LNG and other commodities in the future.

Other structural reform priorities include stimulating private sector investment, particularly outside of the mining sector, increasing competitiveness and diversification. There has been considerable progress in several areas of structural reform in PNG in recent years. In particular, opening markets in telecommunications and air transport in the past two years has produced major welfare gains for the population. Other priorities in the private sector development agenda are maintaining law and order, establishment of a level playing field and improvement in the business climate, especially through opening more markets to competition, commercializing parastatals, reducing the regulatory and licensing burden, clarifying property rights (especially for land). Developing infrastructure – electricity, telecommunications, road and other transport – through private sector involvement and greater efficiency of public investment– will also be important to support growth.

PHILIPPINES

Population	88 million
Population growth	1.9 percent
Surface area	300,000 sq.km.
Capital	Manila

The economy weathered the global crisis comparatively well, escaping a recession, thanks in large part to timely fiscal and monetary stimulus measures and the continued steady inflow of remittances. The authorities now face the challenge of balancing the need to avoid premature withdrawal of fiscal stimulus with ensuring medium-term fiscal consolidation.

After a brief but sharp contraction in early 2009, the economy rebounded moderately in the second quarter in line with consumer spending. Real GDP contracted 2.1 percent in the first quarter of 2009 in seasonally adjusted annualized (SAAR) terms, before expanding 2.4 percent in the second quarter. The contraction in personal consumption expenditure during January-March was the first since the 1980s and underlies the extent of precaution households took when the crisis was in full swing. The recovery in consumption in the second quarter was mostly driven by remittance inflows, declining inflation, and an improving global outlook. Government consumption expanded sharply as well, due to the front loading of the government's fiscal stimulus. Capital formation, however, continued to contract, with sharp falls posted in private construction and durable equipment. Merchandise exports continued to contract on an annual basis in the second quarter, mostly due to smaller shipments of electronics. Export of services, however, expanded, mostly reflecting strong demand abroad for the business process outsourcing (BPO) industry.

The balance of payments surplus rose to $3.3 billion during January-September, thanks to continued larger inflows of remittances and the BPO exports. The rapid growth of the BPO industry in the midst of a global recession stems from continued strong demand for back office, engineering and financial services as corporations across the world seek to optimize their cost structures. The balance of payments surplus boosted foreign exchange reserves to a record high $42.3 billion by the end of September , equivalent to more than seven months of imports and more than three times the country's short-term external debt.

The remarkable resiliency of remittance flows to the Philippines has been surprising but welcome. Growth in monthly remittance flows measured in U.S. dollars slowed sharply during 2009 from double digit increases in 2008, but the expansion of 9.3 percent year-on-year in July compares with declines of 4-20 percent predicted by observers at the start of the year. In real peso terms, moreover, remittances rose by 12 percent year-on-year in January-August after contracting 2.9 percent in 2008. Strong deployment of workers abroad in 2008 and an extensive diversification of the overseas Filipino workers, whether by geographic location, skills, gender, or sectors of activity help explain the resiliency of remittances during the global crisis. Remittances are also expected to play a strong insurance role for families affected by the typhoons that hit the Philippines. The former has severely impact the capital Manila, where most of overseas remittances are sent, and in particular the poor, near-poor and the middle class.

Financial markets have rebounded significantly while real estate prices are contracting moderately. Equity prices rose 46 percent from the start of the year, while spreads on foreign-currency denominated government bonds fell 177 basis points and are only 30 basis points higher than on September 15, 2008. Real estate prices, however, remain under pressure. Land prices in prime Manila locations contracted by

Remittances

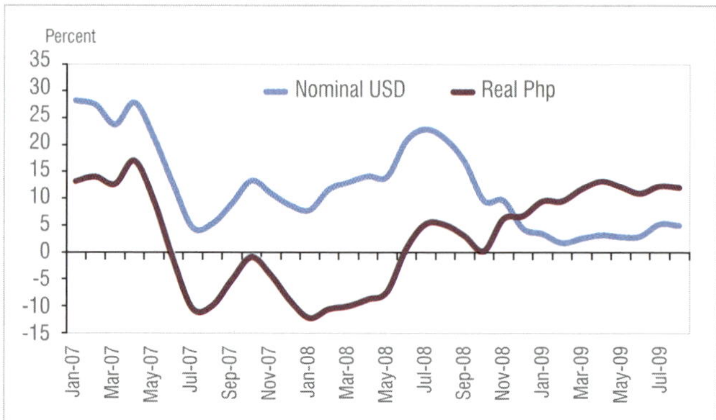

Philippines: Key Indicators

	2006	2007	2008	2009e	2010f	2008		2009		2009			
	Year	Year	Year	Year	Year	Q3	Q4	Q1	Q2	Jun	Jul	Aug	Sep
Output, Employment and Prices													
Real GDP (% change y-y) 1/	5.3	7.1	3.8	1.4	3.1	4.6	2.9	0.6	1.5	..	..	..	..
Industrial production index (1994 = 100)	86.9	84.6	84.8	..	..	88.5	84.6	61.3	71.0	74.0	75.3	..	..
(% change y-y)	-8.5	-2.7	0.3	..	..	4.0	-7.1	-23.3	-17.6	-14.9	-15.8	..	..
Unemployment (%) 2/	8.0	7.3	7.4	..	..	7.4	6.8	7.7	7.5	..	..	..	..
Nominal wages (% change y-y) 3/	7.9	4.5	5.3	..	..	6.7	5.5	5.5	1.8	0.0	0.0	0.0	0.0
Real wages (% change y-y) 3/	0.9	2.0	-1.6	..	..	-1.7	-0.9	1.4	2.9	0.1	1.0	1.1	0.3
Consumer price index (% change y-y)	6.3	2.8	9.3	2.9	4.5	12.2	9.7	6.9	3.2	1.5	0.2	0.1	0.7
Public Sector													
Government balance (% GDP) 4/	-1.4	-1.7	-1.5	-3.8	-3.1	-2.1	-2.0	-7.1	-2.0	..	..	..	..
Domestic public sector debt (% GDP) 5/	31.7	33.1	24.1	..	..	33.5	24.1	..	..	..	..	..	..
Foreign Trade, BOP and External Debt													
Trade balance (billions US$) 6/	-6.7	-8.4	-12.9	-10.8	-12.8	-4.2	-2.2	-2.1	-2.5	-0.7	-0.7	..	..
Exports of goods (billions US$) 6/	46.5	49.5	48.3	39.1	40.3	13.1	10.0	7.7	9.1	3.4	3.3	3.5	..
(% change y-y)	15.6	6.4	-2.5	-19.0	3.0	4.3	-21.9	-37.1	-29.4	-24.5	-25.4	-21.0	..
Key export (% change y-y) 7/	7.5	5.3	-7.2	..	..	-0.3	-26.1	-41.9	-27.6	-25.0	-24.2	-17.0	..
Imports of goods (billions US$) 6/	53.3	57.9	61.1	50.1	53.4	17.3	12.2	9.8	11.5	4.1	4.0	..	..
(% change y-y)	10.9	8.7	5.6	-18.0	6.5	14.6	-20.7	-34.7	-30.4	-22.8	-31.6	..	..
Current account balance (billions US$) 8/	5.3	7.1	3.9	5.4	4.6	-0.4	2.2	1.9	2.0	..	..	..	..
(% GDP)	4.5	4.9	2.3	3.4	2.8	-1.1	5.1	5.2	5.2	..	..	..	..
Foreign direct investment (billions US$)	2.8	-0.6	1.1	0.4	0.5	0.5	0.1	0.0	0.8	..	..	..	..
External debt (billions US$) 9/	53.4	54.9	53.9	..	..	53.5	53.9	52.5	51.8	..	..	..	..
(% GDP)	45.4	38.1	32.3	..	..	32.0	32.3	33.2	32.8	..	..	..	..
Short-term debt (billions US$) 9/	5.0	7.1	7.0	..	..	8.3	7.0	6.5	5.8	..	..	..	..
Debt service (% exports of g&s)	12.0	10.1	9.6	..	..	..	..	..	..	..	..	..	..
Foreign exchange reserves (billions US$) 9/	23.0	33.8	37.6	42.3	44.2	36.7	37.6	39.0	39.5	39.5	40.2	41.5	42.3
(months of imports of g&s) 10/	4.2	5.7	5.7	7.7	7.6	5.6	5.9	6.7	7.3	7.3	7.4	7.7	7.8
Financial Markets													
Domestic credit (% change y-y)	7.2	5.2	16.8	..	..	13.5	16.8	16.0	14.9	14.9	15.0	11.1	..
Short-term interest rate (% p.a.) 11/	7.9	7.2	5.5	..	..	5.7	5.7	5.2	4.6	4.3	4.2	4.1	4.1
Exchange rate (Peso/US$, ave)	51.3	46.1	44.5	..	..	45.5	48.4	47.7	47.9	47.9	48.1	48.2	48.1
Real effective exchange rate (2000=100)	111.1	121.7	128.6	..	..	127.5	110.1	106.0	106.2	124.7	123.8	122.1	120.7
(% change y-y)	11.1	9.6	5.7	..	..	4.6	-13.7	-20.4	-18.1	-2.6	-2.2	-5.8	-4.5
Stock market index (Jan. 2, 1985=100) 12/	2412	3443	2587	..	..	2569	1994	1901	2280	2478	2575	2829	2814
Memo: Nominal GDP (billions US$)	117.5	144.0	166.9	158.1	166.9	40.7	42.9	36.4	39.1	..	..	..	..

Source: National data sources.
f = forecast
1/ The GDP series has a break in 200.
2/ New methodology. The 2003-06 figures are based on 1995 census. The 2007 figure is based on 2000 census.
3/ Non-agriculture wages, National Capital Region.
4/ National government.
5/ Total public sector domestic debt.
6/ Balance-of-payments basis.
7/ Electronics, semiconductors.
8/ Estimate.
9/ Central bank figures.
9/ Includes income receipts
10/ Based on end-of-period gross international reserves. Import cover is average.
11/ Interbank call rate.
12/ PHISIX Composite, period average for annual figures.

3.1 percent in the second quarter from the first, and given existing vacancies and the projected new supplies coming in the market, prices are expected to contract further over the next twelve months.

The fiscal deficit has widened substantially because of the fiscal stimulus package calling for frontloading of spending and noticeably weaker revenues. Spending grew by 15.2 percent from a year earlier in September driven primarily by larger capital spending, wages and transfers to local governments. Tax revenues contracted by 8.5 percent year-on-year in September. About two-thirds of the contraction reflects tax cuts implemented in 2008 and 2009.

Low inflation and a stable exchange rate helped the central bank cut its key policy rate by 200 basis points this year, but the pass-through to bank lending rates has been slow and partial. Inflation declined to 0.1 percent year-on-year in August from a peak of 12.5 percent a year earlier. Bank lending rates, meanwhile, fell only 120 basis points this year. Nonetheless, 12-month growth in bank credit (net of placements in the central bank) slowed to 5.9 percent by August from double digits that prevailed most of 2008.

The adverse impacts of the crisis on the social sector are easing, though the recent typhoons have likely led to renewed duress. As the economy started to recover, "green shoots" emerged in the labor market. The share of wage and salaried workers in total employment increased in July compared to April 2009, offset by a large decline in the number of workers in the informal sector. Hunger incidence also recently receded from its level during the height of the food and global financial crises. Despite these improvements and measures under the government fiscal stimulus package, it is estimated that the global economic recession will leave an additional 1.4 million Filipinos in poverty by 2010 compared with a counterfactual scenario of no crisis. Damages and losses inflicted by the typhoons Ondoy and Pepeng are estimated to worsen poverty incidence even further.

While the country weathered comparatively well the global crisis, important challenges exist for the country to generate inclusive sustainable growth. In particular, there is a need to balance the medium-term need for fiscal consolidation with the risk of a premature unwinding of the fiscal stimulus. Fiscal consolidation is needed to protect and increase priority spending in health, education, and infrastructure, and to help reduce government debt to levels that will open up more fiscal space for the future. Additionally, reaching a higher growth path will require increasing the share of investment in the economy, especially in infrastructure. Improving the business climate is key to achieving this objective. A higher intensity of investment would raise the potential growth rate of the economy and boost incomes, while helping rebalance the economy away from consumption as its key driving force.

SOLOMON ISLANDS

Population	495 thousand
Population growth	2.3 percent
Surface Area	29,000 sq.km.
Capital	Honiara

While the Solomon Islands (Sols) economy has proven relatively resilient over the past decade, weak external conditions along with declining timber production have dampened prospects for growth and export earnings. The relatively strong 2008 GDP growth of 6.9 percent was bolstered by a record harvest of logs, as well as strong demand and record prices for palm oil and copra. However, in 2009, growth is expected to reach only 0.4 percent, dragged heavily by a sharp contraction in the timber sector (the volume of timber exports fell by 32 percent year on year in the first seven months of the year); major floods which adversely affected agricultural production; a weak fisheries sector (the volume of fish production fell by 17 percent year on year in the first seven months of 2009); and falls in commodity prices.

A supportive fiscal stance was targeted in 2009, but periodic cash shortages—in part caused by falling revenues—has at times impeded budget execution. The 2009 budget drawn up in late-2008 assumed that the government would finance an emerging deficit by drawing down its cash balances with the central bank to zero during this year. Unanticipated spending at the end of 2008, coupled with a shortfall in revenues in January, quickly reduced the government's cash reserves, leading the government to take measures over the past few months to conserve cash. These measures included a 10 percent cut in non-essential recurrent outlays, a freeze on civil service hires, an increase in selected import duties and excises, and a tightening of tax and customs exceptions. The fiscal balance is expected to slip into deficit of 0.4 percent of GDP compared to a surplus of 1.5 percent of GDP in 2008.

Growth is expected to recovery very modestly in 2010, but future prospects are damped by the imminent end of large-scale logging. Supported by improving conditions in Sols major East Asian trading partners as well as a rebound in palm oil and copra production, growth is expected to recover modestly to about 2.5 percent in 2010. However, with logging rates above sustainable levels since 1992, log exports are expected to fall by around 80 percent from present rates by 2013. This decline in logging activity is a significant drag on medium-term growth prospects. Mitigating sources of economic growth include the rehabilitation of the Goldridge gold mine, and prospects of nickel mining, from 2012 and 2015 respectively.

The current account is expected to remain under pressure, putting pressure on foreign reserves. Sols has seen a worsening trend in the external accounts where imports have almost doubled as a share of GDP from 27 percent in 2003 to almost 50 percent in 2008, and the current account has moved from broad balance in 2003 to a deficit 19 percent of GDP in 2008. Despite the effects of lower logging production, lower commodity prices have helped provide some cushion to the current account deficit, which is expected to narrow to 11 percent of GDP in 2009. Foreign exchange reserves have been under pressure and fell below 3 months of import cover between October 2008 and March 2009. An uptick in exports in the second quarter (attributed to an increase in the value of log exports) combined with continued decline in imports (due to relatively low food and fuel prices, and lower freight prices) has provided some temporary relief. While reserves now provide over 4 months' import cover, risks remain on the downside.

Solomon Islands: Sources of growth (2006-09)

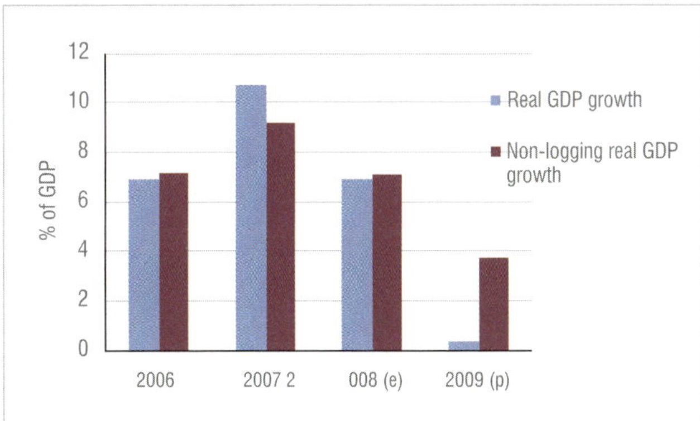

Monetary conditions have tightened and banks have sharply curtailed credit growth due to declines in liquidity and increases in funding costs. Credit growth is projected to decline sharply from 26.5 percent in 2008 to 5 percent in 2009. Inflation is also expected to fall sharply from a peak of 25 percent year-on-year in mid-2008 to around 6 percent by the end of 2009 largely due to lower food and fuel prices.

The immanent end of large scale logging will pose serious economic challenges for the nation and reforms which could generate sources of non-logging economic growth should be given priority. In addition, the government's cash position is under tremendous stress due to lower revenue than forecasted and weakness in cash management, which has resulted in spending in-arrears. Lastly, recent declines in foreign exchange reserves have highlighted the country's external vulnerability, which needs to be addressed in order to promote stability.

THAILAND

Population	64 million
Population growth	0.6 percent
Surface area	513,000 sq.km.
Capital	Bangkok

Thailand's economy is expected to contract by 2.7 percent in 2009, as recovery in the second half of the year helped partly offset the 6 percent decline in real GDP in the first half. Recovery from the impacts of the global economic and financial crisis began around midyear, when exports, industrial production and capacity utilization started a consistent upward trend after plunging in the first half of the year. The recovery is also evident in tighter labor market conditions, as firms have reported difficulties in quickly re-hiring the workers that were let go in the depths of the crisis. (Government policy may have partly contributed to this outcome, as some workers would rather take up government-sponsored training or wait until their unemployment benefits run out). The recovery started later than in other countries in the region in part because of the relatively greater importance of the automotive sector, which has been more sluggish to recover, and in part due to a greater reliance on services exports, which have also lagged.

On the supply side, a contraction in manufacturing drove the large drop in real GDP since late 2008. Manufacturing represents 40 percent of value added, but has accounted for nearly 75 percent of the contraction in real GDP since the onset of the crisis. In just five months between October 2008 and February 2009, capacity utilization fell from about 70 percent to 55 percent (levels close to the troughs following the Asian Financial Crisis), while manufacturing production plummeted by 18 percent over the same period, more than the cumulative decline in 1997-98 over sixteen months. Capacity utilization and manufacturing production showed signs of rebounding starting in April, and by August both indicators were well above their lows, although still depressed compared to pre-crisis levels.

Household consumption grew by a seasonally adjusted 0.8 percent in the second quarter from the first and is likely to have quickened in the remainder of 2009 because of improved consumer sentiment. Household consumption, which is normally the least volatile item of GDP, contracted more than expected in the first half due to a combination of deteriorating employment prospects, declining prices of agricultural goods, and uncertainties from April's political turmoil. Since June, labor market prospects have improved, agricultural prices have stabilized, as did the political situation, thus supporting a pickup in consumption.

The outlook for private investment remains weak relative to the other components of expenditure. Capacity utilization is recovering, but at about 60 percent is still below the historical average of about 70 percent. Moreover, while business sentiment has risen from very low levels, recent results point toward more volatility. Inventories were drawn down substantially in the first half of 2009, but only modest restocking is projected to take place in the remainder of 2009.

Public investment surged in the second quarter, rising 11 percent in seasonally adjusted terms from the first, due to improved disbursements in public construction investments. Given the continued efforts to improve disbursements, as well as the ambitious public investment program under the government's second stimulus package, these large gains

Thailand capacity utilization, seasonally adjusted

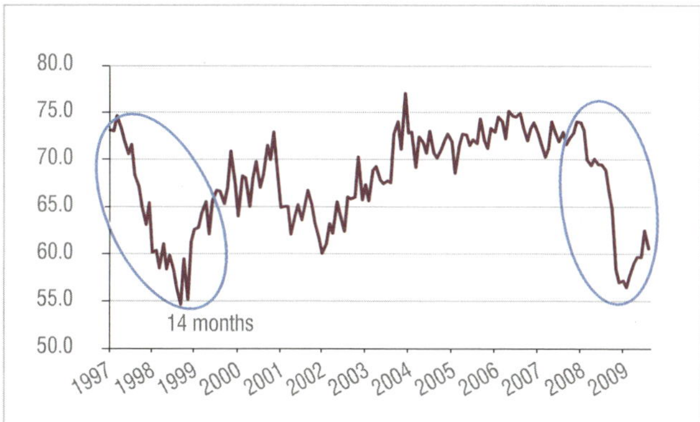

Thailand: Key Indicators

	2006	2007	2008	2009e	2010f	2008		2009		2009			
	Year	Year	Year	Year	Year	Q3	Q4	Q1	Q2	Jun	Jul	Aug	Sep
Output, Employment and Prices													
Real GDP (% change y-y)	5.2	4.9	2.6	-2.7	3.5	3.9	-4.2	-7.1	-4.9	..	..	..	..
Industrial production index (2000=100)	167.0	180.7	190.2	..	..	195.8	176.4	162.5	171.9	179.2	180.3	177.6	..
(% change y-y)	7.3	8.2	5.3	..	..	7.6	-8.1	-18.5	-9.2	-8.3	-7.1	-10.3	..
Unemployment (%)	1.5	1.4	1.4	2.4	2.0	1.2	1.3	2.1	1.7	1.4	1.2	..	..
Real wages (% change y-y) 1/	1.6	0.7	4.8	..	..	1.7	3.6	-6.6	1.1	..	..	..	..
Consumer price index (% change y-y)	4.6	2.2	5.5	0.0	2.0	7.3	2.1	-0.2	-2.8	-4.0	-4.4	-1.0	-1.0
Public Sector													
Government balance (% GDP) 2/	1.1	-1.7	-1.1	-4.2	-4.6	-0.4	-1.1	-2.6	-3.3	..	..	..	..
Domestic public sector debt (% GDP) 3/	34.3	32.9	33.6	..	..	33.2	33.6	37.5	39.0	39.0	40.7	..	..
Foreign Trade, BOP and External Debt													
Trade balance (billions US$)	1.0	11.6	0.2	15.2	10.4	-0.2	-1.4	7.8	3.9	0.9	0.8	2.3	..
Exports of goods (billions US$)	127.9	150.0	175.3	149.9	164.3	49.4	38.3	33.4	34.0	12.2	12.8	13.2	..
(% change y-y)	17.0	17.3	16.8	-14.5	9.6	28.4	-9.4	-19.9	-26.1	-26.4	-26.4	-26.4	..
Key export (% change y-y) 4/	25.2	16.4	7.6	..	..	9.1	-20.1	-31.3	-24.9	-23.1	-20.7	-13.5	..
Imports of goods (billions US$)	126.9	138.5	175.1	134.7	153.9	49.5	39.6	25.6	30.1	11.2	12.0	10.9	..
(% change y-y)	7.9	9.1	26.4	-23.0	14.2	39.1	5.3	-38.3	-32.3	-26.4	-26.4	-26.4	..
Current account balance (billions US$)	2.3	14.5	1.8	17.3	13.0	-0.9	-1.5	9.6	2.8	0.6	0.5	1.9	..
(% GDP)	1.1	5.8	0.6	6.7	4.6	-1.3	-2.4	15.6	4.4	..	..	..	..
Foreign direct investment (billions US$) 5/	10.5	10.3	7.6	6.4	..	2.0	1.5	1.3	1.1	0.5	0.5	0.6	..
External debt (billions US$) 6/	59.6	61.7	67.7	..	..	65.2	64.8	61.5	62.9	..	..	..	..
(% GDP)	28.8	24.9	24.8	..	..	95.2	102.5	99.8	100.5	..	..	..	..
Short-term debt (billions US$) 6/	18.6	21.6	24.1	..	..	25.2	24.1	22.1	21.8	..	..	..	..
Debt service (% exports of g&s)	11.4	11.9	7.1	..	..	5.7	8.0	7.3	6.4	..	..	..	..
Foreign exchange reserves (billions US$)	67.0	87.5	111.0	123.0	..	102.4	111.0	116.2	120.8	120.8	123.4	127.3	131.8
(months of imports of g&s)	6.6	7.9	7.9	11.0	..	5.4	7.1	11.1	10.0	10.0	10.2	10.5	10.9
Financial Markets													
Domestic credit (% change y-y) 7/	4.8	4.9	9.3	..	..	11.2	9.3	6.4	3.2	3.2	2.3	1.3	..
Short-term interest rate (% p.a.) 8/	..	3.69	3.4	1.4	..	3.67	3.42	1.67	1.25	1.25	1.25	1.25	1.25
Exchange rate (Baht/US$, ave)	37.9	34.2	33.4	34.3	33.0	33.9	34.8	35.3	34.7	34.1	34.1	34.0	33.8
Real effective exchange rate (1994=100) 9/	105.3	112.2	112.8	..	..	111.3	109.9	109.4	109.6	109.5	..	..	..
(% change y-y)	7.3	8.2	5.3	..	..	-1.7	-1.5	-4.6	-5.1	-5.0	..	..	..
Stock market index (Dec. 1996=100) 10/	680	858	450.0	..	..	597	450	432	597	597	624	653	717
Memo: Nominal GDP (billions US$)	206.8	248.0	272.9	258.1	283.5	68.5	63.2	61.6	62.6	..	..	..	..

Sources: National data sources, World Bank staff estimates.

f = forecast
1/ Average wage of employed person, using the National Statistical Office Labor Force Survey, deflated by CPI inflation.
2/ Cash balance of central government.
3/ Includes domestic central government (CG) debt, domestic debt of non-financial state enterprises, and the Financial institutions Development Fund (FIDF) debt. Series was revised by adding the Village Fund (VF) and the Energy Fund Public Organization (EFPO).
4/ Machinery and mechanical appliances.
5/ Non-bank FDI.
6/ Bank of Thailand figures.
7/ Private credits from domestically registered commercial banks, branches of foreign banks, international banking facilities, finance companies, specialized banks, thrift and credit cooperatives, and money market mutual funds.
8/ One-day repurchase rate, average.
9/ World Bank staff estimates.
10/ Bangkok SET

in the second quarter are likely to be maintained and public investment should continue to grow strongly in the remainder of 2009. Growth in public consumption should slow in the fourth quarter and into 2010, as the government switches the composition of the fiscal stimulus towards investment measures.

Exports of goods and services started recovering in May. Exports are expected to rise 7-8 percent a quarter in seasonally adjusted terms, mirroring the recorded monthly growth rates in July and August. Exports of services, mostly tourism, are recovering from a low base reflecting the airport closures in the fourth quarter of last year, but recovery is likely to remain subdued. Imports remain weak given only a modest pick-up in investment, consumption and exports. The authorities have limited appreciation of the baht against the dollar to the extent of the appreciation of other regional currencies, resulting in a very stable nominal effective exchange rate.

Substantial uncertainty remains for growth in 2010 given risks to the global outlook. Under the modest recovery in advanced economies assumed in this report, and assuming continued political stability in Thailand, real GDP growth should grow by about 3.5 percent in 2010. About 1-1.5 percentage points of the increase in output will be accounted by inventory accumulation, however. We continue to assume growth converges to potential by 2013, although export growth rates are lower than in recent years given the post-crisis outlook for the global economy.

TIMOR LESTE

Population	1.1 million
Population growth	3.1 percent
Surface area	15,000 sq.km.
Capital	Dili

The global economic crisis has affected Timor-Leste largely through the reduction of oil and natural gas revenues. External linkages through non-energy trade, non-energy investment and financial markets are small. Economic activity remains buoyant on the back of government spending and the relatively large international donor and security presence. External and fiscal balances remain in surplus, although both are projected to narrow significantly in 2009 due to the drop in energy-related revenues and the rapid rise in government spending over the past two years. The deposits of the Petroleum Fund increased by more than 50 percent from a year earlier to $5 billion in July 2009. This provides an important buffer against near-term shocks. The buffer has been supported by continued political stability, just as Timor-Leste celebrated ten years since its vote for independence on August 30. Challenges include ensuring the quality of public spending and improving competitiveness to attract much needed private investment in the non-oil economy.

Economic growth has been high over the past two years, reaching an estimated 12.8 percent in 2008. Data on economic output is limited but indications are that last year's buoyant growth was fuelled by increased private consumption and public investment in infrastructure. The value of imported capital goods (electrical machinery and other equipment used in construction) in the first two quarters of 2009 more than doubled from a year ago. Agricultural output rebounded in 2008 after a drought in 2007. Official statistics show that rice output in 2008 grew by 33 percent and maize output by 40 percent. Other than some limited growth in the tourism and services sector, private sector growth and investment remains constrained by a cycle of low skills, productivity and competitiveness.

Lending to the private sector has stagnated. Credit rose by 0.8 percent on average in the year to June 2009 to $105 million. Total lending to the construction sector has dropped sharply by more than 50 percent since early 2008, but the decline has been offset by increased government construction spending. Lending to the tourism and services sector has increased by nearly 140 percent over the same period. Non-performing loans remain at a high level of about $29 million since 2008. This does not pose a systemic risk because provisions are high; lending to the private sector is limited; the three commercial banks are all branches of foreign banks; and the domestic microfinance institution has capital adequacy well above the required minimum. The spread between lending and deposit rates has narrowed slightly but remains high at around 10 percentage points, reflecting private sector capacity constraints and associated risks.

Lower commodity prices and currency appreciation helped slow inflation from a high of 10.6 percent year-on-year in June 2008. According to official statistics, prices have fallen by 3 percent in the year to June 2009, although the twelve-month average still shows a 5 percent increase. The real effective exchange rate (REER) appreciated sharply from mid-2008 to the first quarter of 2009 but has weakened more recently. The REER does not have a major impact on non-oil exports, which are small and constrained by other factors. Revenues from coffee exports – which account for nearly all non-energy shipments abroad - were up 36 percent from a year earlier, largely reflecting the increase in coffee prices. At the same time, imports of both consumer and capital goods have doubled in the first half of 2009 compared to the same period last year. As a result, the non-oil merchandise trade

Fiscal trends (% of non-oil GDP)

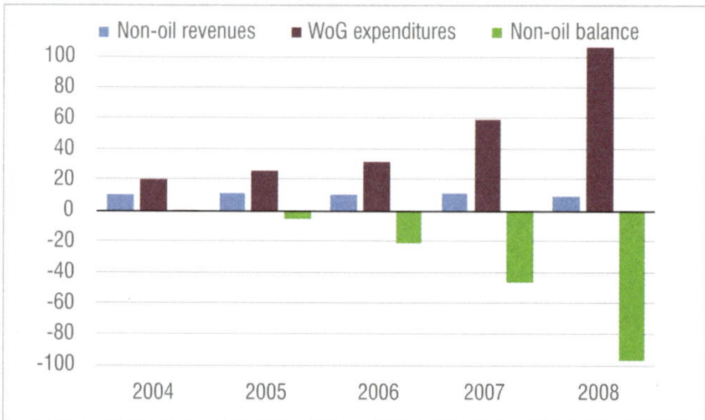

deficit has widened significantly to $168 million in the first half of 2009 from $92 million a year earlier.

Despite the rapidly growing trade deficit, the overall external balance remains strong, supported by the oil and gas sector. Total petroleum receipts for 2009 – that are recorded as service receipts on the balance of payments - are projected to decline due to the drop in oil prices. In 2008, petroleum revenues peaked at $2.4 billion due to high international oil prices and a 15 percent rise in production volumes. Tax and royalty receipts in the second quarter of 2009 dropped by 30 percent compared to the previous quarter and by 35 percent year-on-year. Total revenue for 2009 is projected to amount to $1.46 billion. Foreign direct investment (FDI) outside of the oil and gas sector remains very low. The final 2008 balance of payments statistics show a marked increase in inflows of foreign direct investment to $38 million (7.6 percent of non-oil GDP) from $8.7 million in 2007. Almost all of the increase is for an investment project in the oil and natural gas sector. The Portugal Telecom Group, majority shareholder in Timor Telecom, has indicated its intentions to invest $54 million in 2009 to strengthen the telecommunications network.

Fiscal policy over the past three years has been expansionary, reflecting pressing needs and the government's objectives of promoting social stability and growth. Government expenditures rose from 32 percent of non-oil GDP in 2006 to 106 percent in 2008. Budget execution has improved significantly from 49 percent in 2006 to 80 percent in 2008, as has non-oil revenue collection. The latter remains low, however, at only about 11 percent of non-oil GDP. The overall fiscal balance is in surplus, but is projected to narrow in line with rising spending. The non-oil deficit, meanwhile, is substantial, having increased from 46 percent of non-oil GDP in 2007 to 97 percent in 2008. Whilst this may not be an issue in the short-run, it may lead to less flexibility in the medium term to make fiscal adjustments if oil prices decline anew. Although budgeted spending for 2009 is above the Estimated Sustainable Income (ESI) from the Petroleum Fund, actual withdrawals to date have been within the ESI suggesting expenditure growth may be below the pace budgeted. The draft 2010 budget proposes a slight reduction in planned expenditure compared to 2008, partly through cuts in goods and services and minor capital, and intends to maintain withdrawals from the PF within the ESI.

Parliament recently approved an updated law on Budget and Financial Management. This includes a provision that would allow the government to borrow. Timor-Leste currently has no domestic or external debt. The fiscal deficit is financed entirely out of withdrawals from the Petroleum Fund. Borrowing at concessional rates may make sense if the cost is lower than the foregone income from the Petroleum Fund, taking account of the quality of proposed investments and debt management capacity. The government recently signed a Memorandum of Understanding with the Government of Portugal for a line of credit of up to €100 million per year, but actual borrowing is subject to parliamentary approval. The government is also implementing tax policy and administration reforms introduced in 2008, which contributed to a marked improvement in Timor-Leste's ranking in the 2010 Doing Business report (the country's overall ranking improved to 164th place from 173rd the previous year, but on the ease of paying taxes it surged to 19th place from 75th).

Maintaining fiscal discipline, ensuring the quality of public expenditure and improving productivity and competitiveness are the key challenges. The government has indicated its commitment to maintaining fiscal prudence. This is critical not only for fiscal sustainability, but also for ensuring the quality of spending given its rapid growth in a capacity constrained environment, which increases vulnerability to misuse. Without attention to the quality and prioritization of spending, continued fiscal expansion will have diminishing returns on economic growth. It may also impact adversely on productivity and competitiveness. In light of absorptive capacity constraints, the rise in public spending could create supply bottlenecks leading to inflationary pressures. Improving skills development, targeted investments in critical infrastructure and structural reforms such as liberalization of telecommunications will be important to promoting competitiveness and private investment.

VIETNAM

Population	85 million
Population growth	1.2 percent
Surface area	329,000 sq.km.
Capital	Hanoi

The global financial crisis and economic recession slowed economic growth in Vietnam. The international prices of commodities were on a declining trend since the third quarter of 2008, export orders for garments and other industrial products collapsed in the fourth quarter of 2008, and a slowdown in manufacturing became noticeable. The impact was apparent in the first quarter of 2009, when GDP increased only by 3.1 percent from a year earlier, or 4 percentage points below the average first-quarter growth for the last few years. However, positive signs of recovery have been emerging as a result of the government efforts to support economic activity. The government announced its stimulus package which included various measures, from an interest rate subsidy, to tax breaks, and to additional capital spending. As a result, GDP grew by 4.5 percent in the second quarter and 5.8 percent in the third, raising real GDP growth to 4.6 percent year-on-year for January-September. While manufacturing sector is still facing tough challenges because of falling demand, the construction sector is a leading factor of the recovery, with value-added in the sector projected to reach a double-digit growth rate for the whole year. Domestic consumption is also an important factor of the recovery process, with retail sales increasing 9.3 percent in real terms during January-August from a year earlier. Even though the World Bank's forecasts a growth rate of 5.5 percent for 2009 as a whole, or more than 2 percentage points below the trend, we believe that Vietnam's economy navigated the crisis relatively well.

The global economic recession has had a significant impact on Vietnam's external sector. The main concern is the performance of exports that are equivalent to 70 percent of GDP. Over the first eight months of 2009, exports declined by 14.2 percent year-on-year in dollar terms. Export turnover is down across most items and most of Vietnam's traditional markets. This decline is less than in other developing countries, but could make 2009 the first year with declining exports since the beginning of Vietnam's economic reforms. The decline was even more dramatic for imports which fell 28.2 percent year-on-year in the first eight months of 2009. The relative decline in exports and imports helped narrow the trade deficit and the current account deficit. The latter is projected to be about 5 percent of the GDP in 2009, down from 11.9 percent in 2008. The actual level could be higher if the economy consolidates its current recovery. Although the projected current account deficit should be manageable, foreign exchange reserves declined from $23 billion at the end of 2008 to about $16.5 billion by August 2009. Most of the decline took place between May and July, when the central bank intervened in the exchange rate market to stabilize the currency.

The fiscal deficit is expected to widen to 9.4 percent of GDP in 2009, reflecting a decline in revenues and a significant increase in expenditures. Revenues are projected to fall in line with the slowdown in economic activity, lower oil prices and various tax breaks included in the stimulus packages. Spending is up substantially because of stimulus expenditure measures and the government commitment to social sending to ensure social welfare provision. While Vietnam is able to call for some additional external financing, a sizeable financing gap remains and the government may need to reconsider its stimulus package to maintain the fiscal balance at a manageable level. However, it is noted that the main constraint to support the active fiscal stance of the government stems from short-term financing rather than from medium-term debt sustainability.

Monetary policy has been loosened substantially to support domestic demand after a period of tightening in 2008 to tackle

Exchange rate against the U.S. dollar

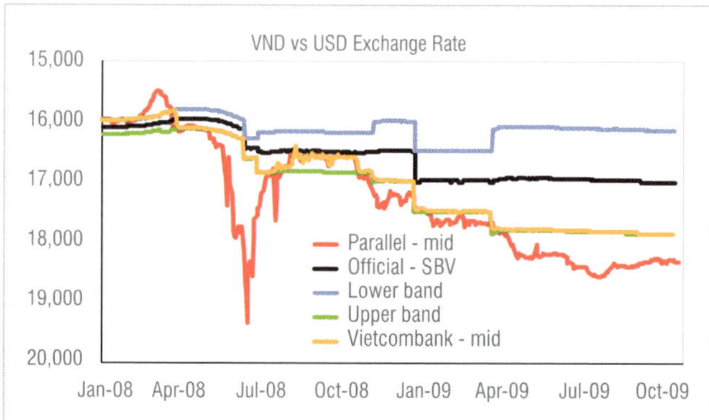

Vietnam: Key Economic Indicators

	2004	2005	2006	2007	2008	2009e
Output, Employment and Prices						
Real GDP (% change y-y)	7.8	8.4	8.2	8.5	6.2	5.5
Industrial production index (% change y-y)	16.0	17.2	17.0	17.1	14.6	14.0
Unemployment (%) 1/	5.6	5.3	4.8	4.6	4.7	5.5
Consumer price index (% change y-y)	7.8	8.3	7.5	12.6	19.9	8.0
Public Sector						
Government balance (% GDP) 2/	0.9	-0.1	1.1	-2.2	-1.6	-4.0
Domestic public sector debt (% GDP) 3/	42.4	44.5	44.1	46.3	44.4	45.8
Foreign Trade, BOP and External Debt						
Trade balance (millions US$)	-5,451	-4,314	-5,065	-14,121	-18,452	-17,044
Exports of goods (millions US$)	26,485	32,447	39,826	48,561	62,685	65,813
(% change y-y)	31.3	22.5	22.7	21.9	29.1	5.0
Key export (% change y-y) 4/	48.3	30.3	12.1	2.7	23.1	-45.0
Imports of goods (millions US$)	31,954	36,761	44,891	62,682	80,416	78,405
(% change y-y)	26.5	15.7	22.1	39.6	28.3	-2.5
Current account balance (millions US$)	-1,591	-561	-229	-6,901	-9,135	-5,210
(% GDP)	-3.5	-1.1	-0.3	-9.9	-10.2	-5.6
Foreign direct investment (billions US$)	1.9	2.0	2.4	6.6	8.1	4.5
External debt (millions US$)	15,600	17,200	19,100	23,700	26,800	28,900
(% GDP)	33.5	32.5	31.4	33.3	29.8	30.9
Debt service (% exports of g&s)	6.0	5.4	5.0	4.6	3.5	4.0
Foreign exchange reserves (millions US$)	6,314	8,557	11,485	21,000	22,400	22,962
(months of imports of g&s)	2.1	2.2	2.1	3.0	4.0	3.5
Financial Markets						
Domestic credit (% change y-y)	41.6	31.7	25.4	53.9	21.0	20.0
Short-term interest rate (% p.a.) 5/	6.7	7.8	7.9	7.4	8.1	6.5
Exchange rate (Dong/US$, eop)	15,777	15,916	16,055	16,010	16,450	17,664
Real effective exchange rate (2000=100)	89.8	93.9	97.3	98.3	110.8	..
(% change y-y)	-1.4	4.5	3.7	1.0	12.7	..
Stock market index (Jul. 2000=100) 6/	239.3	307.5	752.0	972.0	315.6	..
Memo: Nominal GDP (millions US$)	45,428	52,917	60,913	71,034	90,705	93,513

Sources: Vietnam Government Statistics Office, State Bank of Vietnam, IMF, and World Bank staff estimates
e = estimate
f = forecast
1/ Urban areas.
2/ Excludes off-budgetary items.
3/ Includes guaranteed and off-budgetary items.
4/ Crude oil.
5/ Three-month deposit, end-of-period.
6/ Ho Chi Minh Stock Index

overheating. The central bank cut its policy rate by half to 7 percent from mid-2008 to February 2009. The policy rate cut, together with the interest rate subsidy, has led to accelerated bank credit growth. Quantitative indicators of the quality of bank portfolios (based on days in arrears and rollovers) indicate that the fraction of non-performing loans (NPLs) is on the rise. Because the lending rate cannot exceed the policy rate by more than 50 percent, the margins of commercial banks are being seriously squeezed. Low interest rates also make it difficult for the government to issue bonds, and were associated with the reluctance of exporters to sell their foreign exchange. Recognizing emerging risks of the loosening monetary policy, the central bank recently asked largest commercial banks to cap their lending growth at 25 percent this year.

Poverty levels continued to fall in Vietnam, despite the sharp increase in food and fuel prices through the first half of 2008, followed by a period of sluggish growth in late 2008 and into 2009. While poverty fell in aggregate, the economic turbulence of the last two years highlighted a number of new vulnerabilities and continuing challenges. A Participatory Poverty Assessment (PPA) carried out in early 2008 in rural communities underscores Vietnam's considerable recent progress in rural development – PPA respondents noted substantial improvements in rural infrastructure, better access to services, rising agriculture productivity in many regions, and more opportunities to diversify rural income sources. The PPA and related studies also suggest some slow recent progress in poorer regions with high concentrations of ethnic minorities. In addition, rapid assessments of the social impacts of the financial crisis carried out in February and April 2009 highlight growing vulnerabilities among specific populations, including Vietnam's high numbers of migrant workers, workers in the informal sector and household-based enterprises. Greater and more effective investment in education and the training of Vietnam's future workforce will help reduce vulnerabilities, as will the projected strong economic recovery and growing economic opportunities. However, Vietnam's social protection system remains underdeveloped in comparison to many other countries, a gap that will need to be addressed as the country moves forward.

APPENDIX TABLES & CHARTS

Appendix Table 1. Real GDP Growth
(percent change from a year earlier)

	China	Indonesia	Malaysia	Philippines	Thailand	Hong Kong, China	Korea, Rep. of	Singapore	Taiwan, China	East Asia
Q1-2002	8.8	3.5	2.7	4.2	4.5	-1.0	6.6	-0.8	1.3	5.9
Q2-2002	9.2	4.2	4.7	4.6	5.0	0.5	7.0	4.7	4.8	6.8
Q3-2002	9.3	5.6	7.1	3.3	5.8	2.8	6.8	6.5	6.7	7.4
Q4-2002	9.1	4.7	6.9	5.5	6.0	4.8	8.1	6.2	5.7	7.6
Q1-2003	10.8	4.9	6.3	4.8	6.9	4.1	3.5	3.7	3.6	7.3
Q2-2003	8.4	5.0	5.9	4.3	6.6	-0.9	1.8	-1.6	-0.2	5.0
Q3-2003	10.1	4.6	4.6	5.4	6.7	3.8	2.0	4.5	4.1	6.7
Q4-2003	10.4	4.6	6.5	5.1	8.3	4.7	3.9	8.5	6.3	7.6
Q1-2004	9.8	4.1	8.2	7.2	6.7	7.7	5.2	9.6	8.0	8.0
Q2-2004	9.6	4.4	7.9	7.1	6.6	12.0	5.9	13.0	9.2	8.5
Q3-2004	9.2	4.5	6.4	5.6	6.3	6.6	4.8	7.7	5.4	7.2
Q4-2004	9.5	7.2	4.9	5.8	5.9	7.9	2.7	7.2	2.5	6.8
Q1-2005	10.5	6.0	5.6	4.5	3.6	6.2	2.7	4.3	2.2	7.0
Q2-2005	10.5	5.9	4.3	5.1	4.7	7.1	3.4	6.7	3.1	7.3
Q3-2005	10.2	5.8	5.6	4.7	5.5	8.1	4.5	8.8	4.4	7.7
Q4-2005	10.4	5.1	5.9	5.4	4.7	6.9	5.1	9.3	6.9	8.0
Q1-2006	10.4	5.1	6.0	5.5	6.4	9.0	6.1	10.6	5.0	8.3
Q2-2006	11.5	4.9	6.1	5.3	5.3	6.1	5.1	8.3	4.9	8.4
Q3-2006	10.6	5.9	5.8	5.2	4.8	6.4	5.0	7.7	5.5	8.0
Q4-2006	10.4	6.1	5.4	5.4	4.5	6.7	4.6	7.0	3.9	7.7
Q1-2007	11.1	6.0	5.4	6.9	4.4	5.6	4.5	7.6	3.8	8.1
Q2-2007	11.9	6.6	5.6	8.3	4.4	6.1	5.3	8.6	5.5	8.9
Q3-2007	11.5	6.6	6.5	6.8	5.1	6.8	4.9	9.5	7.0	8.9
Q4-2007	11.2	5.8	7.2	6.3	5.7	6.9	5.7	5.5	6.4	8.7
Q1-2008	10.6	6.2	7.4	3.9	6.0	7.3	5.5	6.7	6.2	8.4
Q2-2008	10.1	6.4	6.6	4.2	5.3	4.1	4.3	2.5	4.6	7.5
Q3-2008	9.0	6.4	4.8	4.6	3.9	1.5	3.1	0.0	-1.0	6.0
Q4-2008	6.8	5.2	0.1	2.9	-4.2	-2.6	-3.4	-4.2	-8.6	2.3
Q1-2009	6.1	4.4	-6.2	0.6	-7.1	-7.8	-4.2	-9.5	-10.1	0.9
Q2-2009	7.9	4.0	-3.9	1.5	-4.9	-3.8	-2.2	-3.5	-7.5	2.9
Q3-2009	8.9	..	..	..	..	..	0.6	0.8	..	..

Sources: Haver Analytics and national sources.

Quarterly data for China is estimated using new annual production side GDP data.

Appendix Table 2. Real GDP and Components of Aggregate Demand

(percent change from a year earlier)

		Indonesia	Malaysia	Philippines	Thailand	Hong Kong China	Korea, Rep. of	Singapore	Taiwan, China	S.E. Asia	NIEs
GDP	2005	5.7	5.3	5.0	4.6	7.1	4.0	7.3	4.2	5.2	5.2
	2006	5.5	5.9	5.3	5.2	7.0	5.2	8.4	4.8	5.5	5.6
	2007	6.3	6.2	7.1	4.9	6.4	5.1	7.8	5.7	6.0	5.9
	2008	6.1	4.6	3.8	2.6	2.4	2.2	1.2	0.1	4.5	4.2
	Q1 2009	4.4	-6.3	0.6	-7.1	-7.8	-4.3	-9.5	-10.1	-1.4	-4.2
	Q2 2009	4.0	-3.9	1.5	-4.9	-3.8	-2.2	-3.5	-7.5	-0.4	-2.4
	Q3 2009	..	..	..	..	..	0.6	0.8	..	..	..
Private Consumption	2005	4.0	9.1	4.8	4.6	3.0	4.6	3.8	3.0	5.3	6.7
	2006	3.2	6.8	5.5	3.0	5.9	4.7	4.0	1.8	4.2	5.1
	2007	5.0	10.4	5.9	1.6	8.5	5.1	5.2	2.3	5.3	6.7
	2008	5.3	8.5	4.7	2.5	1.5	0.9	2.4	-0.3	5.1	6.0
	Q1 2009	6.0	-0.7	1.3	-2.5	-6.0	-4.4	-4.3	-1.4	1.6	0.0
	Q2 2009	4.8	0.5	2.3	-2.3	-1.0	-0.8	-3.7	0.4	1.6	0.6
	Q3 2009	..	..	..	..	..	0.6	..	..	..	..
Fixed Investment	2005	10.9	5.0	-6.6	10.5	4.1	1.9	-0.1	1.2	6.7	6.5
	2006	2.6	7.5	3.9	3.9	7.1	3.4	13.3	0.9	4.1	5.4
	2007	9.4	9.6	10.9	1.3	3.4	4.2	19.2	1.9	7.5	7.3
	2008	11.7	0.8	2.9	1.1	-0.5	-1.7	13.7	-10.6	5.3	2.8
	Q1 2009	3.4	-10.8	-7.2	-15.8	-13.7	-8.1	-15.1	-33.4	-6.3	-9.6
	Q2 2009	2.7	-9.8	-1.9	-10.1	-14.0	-2.7	-7.2	-23.7	-4.0	-7.2
	Q3 2009	..	..	..	..	..	-1.4	..	..	..	..
Exports of Goods & Services	2005	16.6	8.3	4.8	4.2	10.6	7.8	12.3	7.6	9.6	8.1
	2006	9.4	7.0	13.4	9.2	9.4	11.4	11.7	10.3	9.5	8.5
	2007	8.5	4.5	5.4	7.1	8.3	12.6	8.7	8.8	6.8	5.9
	2008	9.5	1.3	-1.9	5.4	2.7	5.7	1.3	0.0	4.9	3.5
	Q1 2009	-18.7	-15.2	-14.7	-16.7	-19.3	-10.6	-21.1	-27.2	-16.8	-16.1
	Q2 2009	-15.7	-17.3	-15.9	-21.8	-11.2	-3.9	-15.7	-18.4	-17.7	-18.2
	Q3 2009	..	..	..	..	..	0.9	..	..	..	..

Sources: Haver Analytics, national data sources, and World Bank staff estimates. Regional averages are 2000 US$ GDP weighted.

Appendix Table 3: East Asia: Merchandise Export Growth

(in U.S. dollars, percent change from a year earlier)

	2007	2008	Q3 2008	Q4 2008	Q1 2009	Q2 2009	Q3 2009	Jun-09	Jul-09	Aug-09	Sep-09
East Asia (10)	16.9	13.6	20.4	-4.7	-24.5	-24.0	..	-20.7	-23.5	-21.3	..
China	25.7	17.3	23.3	4.4	-19.7	-23.4	-20.5	-21.2	-22.8	-23.4	-15.2
S.E. Asia	13.3	15.0	24.3	-9.6	-25.6	-26.9	..	-24.7	-26.2	-19.8	..
Indonesia	13.2	20.1	27.9	-5.6	-31.9	-26.2	..	-26.8	-22.7	-15.4	..
Malaysia	9.7	13.3	21.3	-12.6	-28.9	-33.3	..	-28.4	-29.3	-24.0	..
Philippines	7.1	-2.8	4.0	-22.5	-36.8	-28.9	..	-24.8	-25.4	-21.0	..
Thailand	16.5	15.7	26.7	-10.0	-23.2	-23.6	-16.7	-22.7	-25.1	-17.2	-7.2
Vietnam	25.0	25.9	39.9	5.7	4.1	-14.7	..	-13.9	-26.6	-21.9	..
NIEs	10.9	9.3	15.8	-11.5	-28.4	-23.3	..	-18.3	-23.0	-19.6	..
Hong Kong, China	8.8	5.3	5.6	-1.8	-21.5	-12.4	..	-4.7	-19.4	-13.3	..
Korea, Rep. of	14.1	13.6	27.0	-9.9	-25.2	-20.5	-16.6	-12.5	-21.9	-20.9	-6.6
Singapore	10.1	12.9	21.0	-14.0	-32.8	-30.7	-22.2	-28.6	-27.3	-20.7	-18.2
Taiwan, China	10.3	3.7	8.0	-25.0	-37.1	-32.5	-20.8	-30.7	-24.1	-24.7	-12.7

Sources: Haver Analytics and national data sources.

Appendix Table 4. East Asia and the Pacific: Real GDP Growth Projections

(percent change from a year earlier)

	2002	2003	2004	2005	2006	2007	2008	Forecast 2009	Forecast 2010
East Asia	6.9	6.8	7.9	7.6	8.6	9.4	6.0	3.9	6.4
Developing East Asia	7.9	8.8	9.0	9.1	10.2	11.4	8.0	6.7	7.5
China	9.1	10.0	10.1	10.4	11.6	13.0	9.0	8.4	8.7
Indonesia	4.4	4.7	5.0	5.7	5.5	6.3	6.1	4.3	5.4
Malaysia	5.4	5.8	6.8	5.3	5.8	6.3	4.6	-2.3	4.1
Philippines	4.3	5.0	6.4	5.0	5.4	7.2	4.6	1.4	3.1
Thailand	5.3	7.1	6.3	4.5	5.1	4.8	2.6	-2.7	3.5
Vietnam	7.1	7.3	7.8	8.4	8.2	8.5	6.2	5.5	6.5
Cambodia	6.5	8.5	10.0	13.5	10.8	10.2	6.7	-2.2	4.2
Lao PDR	5.9	6.1	6.4	7.1	8.1	7.6	7.3	6.4	7.5
Timor Leste	2.4	0.1	4.2	6.2	-5.8	8.4	12.8	7.4	8.0
Mongolia	4.2	6.1	10.8	7.1	8.6	9.9	8.9	0.5	3.0
Fiji	3.2	1.0	5.3	0.7	3.6	-6.6	0.2	-0.3	1.8
Papua New Guinea	-0.2	2.2	2.7	3.4	2.6	6.2	6.6	3.9	3.7
East Asia NIEs	5.3	3.2	6.1	4.9	5.6	5.6	1.7	-2.2	4.0
Hong Kong, China	1.8	3.0	8.5	7.1	7.0	6.4	2.5	-3.0	3.7
Korea, Rep. of	7.0	3.1	4.7	4.2	5.1	5.0	2.2	-0.7	3.7
Singapore	4.2	3.5	9.0	7.3	8.2	7.7	2.5	-2.6	4.3
Taiwan, China	4.6	3.5	6.2	4.2	4.9	5.7	0.1	-3.8	4.5

Sources: World Bank data and staff estimates.

Appendix Table 5. Regional Aggregates for Poverty Measures in East Asia

		$1.25 –a-day		$2-a-day		
	Mean Consumption (2005 PPP$/ month)	Headcount Index (%)	Number of Poor (million)	Headcount Index (%)	Number of Poor (million)	Population (million)
EAP						
1990	49.16	54.7	873.3	79.8	1,273.7	1,595.9
1993	54.55	50.8	845.3	75.8	1,262.1	1,664.9
1996	67.01	36.0	622.3	64.1	1,108.1	1,728.7
1999	70.76	35.5	635.1	61.8	1,104.9	1,788.4
2002	85.65	27.6	506.8	51.9	954.1	1,837.0
2005	106.85	16.8	316.2	38.7	728.7	1,884.4
EAP excluding China						
1990	72.98	39.2	180.5	66.0	304.4	460.8
1993	73.84	42.6	207.3	68.0	330.9	486.4
1996	85.81	35.0	178.8	61.5	314.2	511.2
1999	82.96	35.2	188.1	62.7	335.2	534.7
2002	89.76	25.5	142.1	54.0	300.8	556.6
2005	100.98	19.0	110.2	44.8	259.5	579.9
South East Asia (Indonesia, Malaysia, Philippines, Thailand)						
1990	77.05	38.6	120.3	65.1	202.9	311.8
1993	82.24	37.8	124.2	63.8	209.8	328.7
1996	96.46	29.5	101.6	56.2	193.9	344.9
1999	91.12	31.8	114.8	59.2	213.6	361.1
2002	97.84	21.3	80.3	49.9	188.4	377.3
2005	107.30	17.0	66.8	42.2	166.0	393.8
Lower-Income East Asia (Cambodia, Lao PDR, PNG, Vietnam)						
1990	58.57	41.2	34.6	69.5	58.4	84.1
1993	43.53	60.5	54.4	83.6	75.2	90.0
1996	47.82	55.1	52.7	80.6	77.1	95.7
1999	54.43	47.3	47.4	75.3	75.6	100.3
2002	60.87	41.0	42.6	69.1	71.9	104.1
2005	79.14	26.1	28.4	53.8	58.6	108.8

Source: World Bank staff estimates.

Appendix Table 6. Primary Commodity Prices

(in U.S. dollars, percent change from a year earlier)

			Actual									Projections	
Commodity	1980-90	1991-98	2000	2001	2002	2003	2004	2005	2006	2007	2008	2009	2010
Crude oil average	0.0	-5.7	56.2	-13.7	2.4	15.9	30.6	41.5	20.4	10.6	36.4	-37.0	19.9
Non-Energy Commodities	-0.8	0.4	-1.4	-9.1	5.3	10.2	17.5	12.0	29.0	17.1	21.0	-32.0	-2.5
Agriculture	-1.9	0.8	-5.7	-9.1	8.6	9.6	10.5	2.8	12.6	20.1	27.2	-23.4	-1.2
Cocoa	-7.3	4.0	-20.2	18.0	66.4	-1.5	-11.5	-0.8	3.5	22.6	32.0	4.8	-11.1
Coffee, arabica	-3.6	12.6	-16.2	-28.5	-1.2	4.3	25.3	42.7	-0.4	8.0	13.1	-5.9	-6.9
Coconut oil	-1.4	10.6	-38.9	-29.4	32.4	11.0	41.4	-6.6	-1.6	51.4	33.2	-42.8	7.1
Palm oil	-3.0	12.3	-28.8	-7.9	36.6	13.6	6.3	-10.4	13.3	63.1	21.6	-31.5	1.5
Rice, Thai, 5%	0.8	2.1	-18.5	-14.6	11.0	3.0	20.3	20.4	6.5	7.1	99.2	-14.6	-17.1
Sugar, world	16.4	-2.8	30.6	5.6	-20.3	3.0	1.1	37.9	49.5	-31.8	27.0	24.1	-17.1
Logs, Malaysia	1.9	3.4	1.5	-16.3	2.7	14.5	5.4	3.0	17.9	11.9	9.1	-0.8	-5.2
Sawn wood, Malaysia	4.1	-0.1	-1.0	-19.1	9.4	4.6	5.5	13.4	13.6	7.6	10.3	-10.6	-4.4
Rubber, RSS1, Sgp	-1.7	0.5	6.2	-13.8	33.0	41.5	20.4	15.2	40.3	8.7	12.9	-38.1	0.0
Metals and minerals	2.9	-2.6	12.6	-9.6	-3.1	12.7	37.1	28.9	56.9	12.0	3.7	-42.8	1.4
Tin	-6.7	-0.7	0.6	-17.5	-9.5	20.5	73.9	-13.3	19.0	65.6	27.3	-29.8	7.7
Copper	4.3	-4.1	15.3	-13.0	-1.2	14.1	61.1	28.4	82.7	5.9	-2.3	-28.1	10.0

Source: World Bank DEC Prospects Group. Projections as of 8/27/09.

Appendix Table 7. East Asia: Exchange Rates
(local currency per U.S. dollar, end-of-period)

	China	Indonesia	Malaysia	Philippines	Thailand	Vietnam	Hong Kong, China	Korea, Rep. of	Singapore	Taiwan, China	Japan
Jan-2007	7.78	9090	3.50	49.03	35.80	16035.50	7.81	940.90	1.54	32.95	121.68
Feb-2007	7.74	9160	3.51	48.29	35.45	15990.00	7.81	938.30	1.53	32.95	118.48
Mar-2007	7.73	9118	3.46	48.26	35.02	16022.50	7.81	940.30	1.52	33.09	117.65
Apr-2007	7.71	9083	3.42	47.51	34.77	16045.50	7.82	929.40	1.52	33.28	119.60
May-2007	7.65	8828	3.40	46.27	34.65	16079.00	7.81	929.90	1.53	33.02	121.62
Jun-2007	7.62	9054	3.45	46.33	34.54	16113.00	7.81	926.80	1.53	32.74	123.23
Jul-2007	7.57	9186	3.45	45.61	33.81	16126.50	7.83	923.20	1.51	32.81	118.95
Aug-2007	7.56	9410	3.50	46.70	34.33	16225.50	7.80	939.90	1.52	33.00	116.20
Sep-2007	7.51	9137	3.42	45.06	34.27	16091.50	7.77	920.70	1.49	32.58	115.05
Oct-2007	7.47	9103	3.34	43.95	34.00	16082.50	7.75	907.40	1.45	32.41	114.75
Nov-2007	7.40	9376	3.36	42.80	33.85	16044.00	7.79	929.60	1.45	32.27	110.30
Dec-2007	7.30	9419	3.31	41.40	33.75	16010.00	7.80	938.20	1.44	32.44	114.00
Jan-2008	7.19	9291	3.24	40.65	33.03	15971.00	7.80	943.90	1.42	32.20	106.36
Feb-2008	7.11	9051	3.19	40.36	31.87	15931.00	7.78	937.30	1.39	30.95	104.73
Mar-2008	7.02	9217	3.19	41.87	31.51	16105.00	7.79	991.70	1.38	30.41	100.10
Apr-2008	7.00	9234	3.16	42.19	31.74	16116.00	7.80	999.70	1.36	30.45	104.08
May-2008	6.95	9318	3.24	43.88	32.46	16246.00	7.80	1031.40	1.37	30.41	105.66
Jun-2008	6.86	9225	3.27	44.76	33.52	16842.00	7.80	1043.40	1.36	30.35	106.40
Jul-2008	6.86	9118	3.26	44.14	33.54	16755.00	7.80	1008.50	1.37	30.59	107.99
Aug-2008	6.85	9157	3.39	45.69	34.17	16525.00	7.80	1081.80	1.42	31.52	109.10
Sep-2008	6.85	9378	3.46	46.92	34.02	16575.00	7.77	1187.70	1.43	32.13	104.30
Oct-2008	6.86	10995	3.56	48.75	34.99	16812.50	7.75	1291.40	1.48	33.00	98.30
Nov-2008	6.87	12151	3.62	48.88	35.47	16973.50	7.75	1482.70	1.51	33.30	95.25
Dec-2008	6.86	10950	3.46	47.49	34.93	17433.00	7.75	1257.50	1.44	32.86	90.75
Jan-2009	6.86	11355	3.61	47.08	34.93	17474.50	7.75	1368.50	1.51	33.80	89.60
Feb-2009	6.84	11980	3.69	48.24	36.05	17475.00	7.75	1516.40	1.54	34.95	97.55
Mar-2009	6.84	11575	3.65	48.42	35.52	17756.00	7.75	1377.10	1.52	33.92	98.10
Apr-2009	6.85	10713	3.56	48.70	35.30	17784.00	7.75	1348.00	1.48	33.23	97.60
May-2009	6.82	10340	3.51	47.55	34.38	17784.00	7.75	1272.90	1.45	32.65	96.50
Jun-2009	6.81	10225	3.53	48.31	34.02	17801.00	7.75	1284.70	1.45	32.82	95.95
Jul-2009	6.82	9920	3.52	48.12	34.04	17815.00	7.75	1240.50	1.44	32.82	95.33
Aug-2009	6.82	10060	3.53	48.91	34.01	17823.00	7.75	1244.90	1.44	32.92	92.70
Sep-2009	6.83	9681	3.47	47.59	33.55	17841.00	7.75	1188.70	1.41	32.20	89.77

Sources: Haver Analytics, Datastream.

Appendix Table 8. East Asia: Foreign Reserves Minus Gold
(in billions of U.S. dollars)

	China	Indonesia	Malaysia	Philippines	Thailand	Hong Kong, China	Korea, Rep. of	Singapore	Taiwan, China	Total
Dec-1997	142.8	17.4	20.8	7.3	26.3	92.8	20.4	71.3	83.5	482.5
Dec-1998	149.2	23.5	25.6	9.3	28.8	89.7	52.0	75.1	90.3	543.4
Dec-1999	157.7	27.3	30.6	13.3	34.1	96.2	74.0	77.0	106.2	616.4
Dec-2000	168.3	29.4	29.5	13.1	32.0	107.5	96.1	80.2	106.7	662.9
Dec-2001	215.6	28.0	30.5	13.5	32.4	111.2	102.8	75.7	122.2	731.7
Dec-2002	291.1	32.0	34.2	13.3	38.1	111.9	121.3	82.2	161.7	885.9
Dec-2003	408.2	36.3	44.6	13.7	41.1	118.4	155.3	96.2	206.6	1,120.3
Dec-2004	614.5	36.3	66.4	13.1	48.7	123.5	199.0	112.6	241.7	1,455.9
Dec-2005	821.5	34.7	70.2	15.9	50.7	124.2	210.3	116.2	253.3	1,697.1
Dec-2006	1,068.5	42.6	82.2	20.0	65.3	133.2	238.9	136.3	266.1	2,053.0
Dec-2007	1,530.3	56.9	101.1	30.2	85.2	152.6	262.2	163.0	270.3	2,651.7
Dec-2008	1,949.3	51.6	91.2	33.2	108.7	182.5	201.2	174.0	291.7	3,083.3
Jan-2009	1,916.6	50.9	91.0	34.7	108.2	181.7	201.7	166.9	292.7	3,044.3
Feb-2009	1,915.1	50.6	90.7	34.2	110.7	177.0	201.5	163.3	294.2	3,037.5
Mar-2009	1,956.8	54.8	87.4	34.5	113.7	186.2	206.3	166.0	300.1	3,106.1
Apr-2009	2,012.0	56.6	87.8	34.9	114.4	193.4	212.5	169.9	304.7	3,186.1
May-2009	2,093.1	57.9	87.9	34.7	118.9	205.1	226.8	171.5	312.6	3,308.5
Jun-2009	2,135.2	57.6	91.3	34.8	118.3	206.9	231.7	173.0	317.6	3,366.4
Jul-2009	2,178.2	57.4	90.8	35.3	120.9	218.0	237.5	173.9	321.1	3,433.2
Aug-2009	2,223.9	57.9	93.3	36.7	124.8	223.3	245.5	176.1	325.4	3,506.7
Sep-2009		62.3	94.7	37.5	129.1	226.9	254.2	181.8	332.2	

Sources: Haver Analytics, Thomson Datastream, and IMF International Financial Statistics.

Table 9a. East Asia: Balance of Payments

(in percent of GDP)

	Overall Balance 1/					Current Account					Capital Account 2/				
	2005	2006	2007	2008	2009*	2005	2006	2007	2008	2009*	2005	2006	2007	2008	2009*
East Asia	5.4	6.7	9.5	5.9	4.9	5.7	7.4	8.5	7.4	7.4	-0.3	-0.6	1.0	-1.5	-2.5
China 3/	9.0	8.9	13.3	9.5	7.2	7.0	9.1	10.7	9.6	8.2	2.0	-0.2	2.6	1.2	-1.0
S.E. Asia	1.0	4.6	6.3	1.0	-1.7	2.2	5.3	6.0	3.7	4.9	-1.2	-0.7	0.2	-4.0	-6.6
Indonesia	-0.6	2.2	3.3	-1.0	-0.4	0.1	3.0	2.4	0.1	0.9	-0.6	-0.8	0.9	-1.9	-1.2
Malaysia	2.7	7.6	10.1	-4.5	-17.3	15.0	16.7	15.7	17.6	18.6	-12.3	-9.1	-5.6	-23.0	-35.9
Philippines	2.8	3.5	7.0	1.8	1.3	1.9	4.4	5.0	2.5	3.6	0.9	-1.0	2.1	-1.8	-2.3
Thailand	1.1	7.1	8.1	8.6	5.9	-4.3	1.1	5.7	-0.1	3.2	5.5	5.9	2.4	5.4	2.7
NIEs	1.8	4.3	4.1	0.1	2.9	5.3	5.5	5.7	4.4	6.8	-3.5	-1.2	-1.7	-6.7	-3.9
Hong Kong, China	0.4	4.7	9.4	13.9	23.4	11.4	12.1	12.3	14.2	14.9	-11.0	-7.4	-2.9	-1.0	8.5
Korea, Rep. of	1.3	3.0	2.2	-6.5	-3.3	1.8	0.5	0.5	-0.4	2.6	-0.4	2.5	1.7	-9.0	-5.8
Singapore	3.0	14.4	16.0	6.1	-2.2	22.7	25.4	23.4	14.9	12.6	-19.7	-11.0	-7.4	-6.5	-14.7
Taiwan, China	3.2	3.5	1.1	5.5	7.1	4.9	7.1	8.5	6.4	8.7	-1.7	-3.6	-7.4	-3.2	-1.6
Median	2.7	4.7	8.1	5.5	1.3	4.9	7.1	8.5	6.4	8.2	-0.6	-1.0	0.9	-1.9	-1.6

Sources: Haver Analytics, national sources.

1/ Equals change in foreign reserves.

2/ Includes errors and omissions.

* Four-quarter total, 3Q 2008 - 2Q 2009

Table 9b. East Asia: Capital Account Components

(in percent of GDP)

	Net FDI					Net Portfolio					Net Other Capital 3/				
	2005	2006	2007	2008	2009*	2005	2006	2007	2008	2009*	2005	2006	2007	2008	2009*
East Asia	2.0	1.6	1.8	1.3	1.2	-0.7	-2.4	-0.8	-1.1	-0.9	-0.6	0.1	-1.2	-1.1	-1.9
China 3/	2.9	2.2	3.5	2.1	1.7	-0.2	-2.4	0.5	1.0	0.9	-0.2	0.5	-2.0	-2.7	-3.0
S.E. Asia	2.2	1.6	0.7	0.2	0.2	1.4	1.8	0.9	-2.8	-3.5	-3.1	-3.7	-2.4	0.3	-2.2
Indonesia	1.8	0.6	0.5	0.5	0.8	1.5	1.2	1.3	0.3	-0.1	-3.3	-1.0	-1.1	-1.2	-1.4
Malaysia	0.7	0.0	-1.4	-3.5	-3.9	-2.7	2.2	2.9	-11.4	-16.2	-5.1	-9.8	-7.3	-1.1	-7.1
Philippines	1.7	2.4	-0.4	0.7	0.9	3.5	2.6	3.2	-2.3	-1.8	-3.0	-5.1	-0.3	0.4	-1.5
Thailand	4.3	4.1	3.5	2.2	1.6	3.1	2.1	-2.7	-2.1	-1.4	-1.1	-2.9	-2.2	4.1	-0.3
NIEs	0.5	0.6	-0.9	0.1	0.5	-2.5	-4.5	-4.3	-5.1	-4.0	0.0	1.4	1.0	2.3	1.7
Hong Kong, China	3.6	0.0	-3.3	1.4	1.9	-17.7	-14.1	-1.3	-17.4	-17.3	2.0	3.2	-5.0	17.9	23.2
Korea, Rep. of	0.2	-0.5	-1.3	-1.1	-0.5	-0.4	-2.4	-2.5	-5.7	1.1	0.8	5.1	4.2	-1.1	-3.3
Singapore	2.6	10.3	4.2	7.6	5.9	0.8	-3.7	-5.7	-12.7	-15.3	-18.0	-22.3	-11.8	-1.0	-3.2
Taiwan, China	-1.2	0.0	-0.9	-1.2	-0.6	-0.8	-5.2	-10.4	-3.2	-2.3	3.0	0.1	1.2	3.6	2.6
Median	1.8	0.6	-0.4	0.7	0.9	-0.2	-2.4	-1.3	-3.2	-1.8	-1.1	-1.0	-2.0	-1.0	-1.5

Sources: Haver Analytics, national sources.

3/ Net Other Investment + Financial Derivatives

* Four-quarter total, 3Q 2008 - 2Q 2009

Appendix Table 10. East Asia: Nonperforming Loans
(in percent of total loans)

	1997	1998	1999	2000	2001	2002	2003	2004	2005	2006	2007	2008	2009		
	Dec	Dec	Dec	Dec	Dec	Dec	Dec	Dec	Dec	Dec	Dec	Dec	Mar	Jun	Sep
China	..	..	..	..	..	23.1	17.9	13.2	8.6	7.1	6.2	2.4	2.0	1.8	1.7
Indonesia 1/	7.2	48.6	32.9	18.8	12.1	7.5	6.8	4.5	7.6	6.1	5.2	3.9	4.3	4.6	..
Malaysia 2/	..	10.6	11.0	9.7	11.5	10.2	9.0	7.5	5.8	4.8	3.2	2.2	2.2	2.2	2.1
Philippines 3/	..	11.0	12.7	14.9	16.9	14.6	13.8	12.5	8.6	6.1	4.9	4.1	4.3	..	..
Thailand 4/	..	45.0	39.9	19.5	11.5	18.1	13.9	11.6	8.3	8.1	7.3	5.3	5.5	5.4	5.3
Korea, Rep. of 5/	6.0	7.3	13.6	8.8	3.3	2.4	2.2	2.0	1.3	0.9	0.7	1.1	1.47	1.5	..

Source: National data sources.

1/ Excludes IBRA's AMC.

2/ Excludes Danaharta. This series, used by Bank Negara Malaysia, is net of provisions and excludes interest in suspense.

3/ Includes interbank loans.

4/ Excludes transfers to AMCs. The jump in headline NPLs in December 2002 was a one-off increase, reflecting a change in definition and did not affect provisioning.

5/ Excludes KAMCO/KDIC.

Appendix Table 11. East Asia: Financial Market Indicators

Stock Market Index, end-of-period, Dec. 31, 2007 = 100

	Sep-07	Dec-07	Mar-08	Jun-08	Sep-08	Dec-08	Mar-09	Jun-09	Sep-09
China	105.5	100.0	66.0	52.0	43.6	34.6	45.1	56.3	52.8
Indonesia	85.9	100.0	89.1	85.6	66.7	49.4	52.2	73.8	89.9
Malaysia	92.5	100.0	86.3	82.1	70.5	60.7	60.4	74.4	83.2
Philippines	98.7	100.0	82.4	67.9	71.0	51.7	54.8	67.3	77.3
Thailand	98.5	100.0	95.2	89.6	69.5	52.4	50.3	69.6	83.6
Vietnam	112.9	100.0	55.8	43.1	49.3	34.0	30.3	48.4	62.7
Hong Kong, China	97.6	100.0	82.2	79.5	64.8	51.7	48.8	66.1	75.3
Korea, Rep. of	102.6	100.0	89.8	88.3	76.3	59.3	63.6	73.3	88.2
Singapore	105.2	100.0	86.8	85.1	68.1	50.8	49.1	67.3	77.1
Taiwan, China	110.6	100.0	100.8	88.4	67.2	54.0	61.3	75.6	88.3

Source: Thomson Datastream.

Yields, 10-year local-currency government bonds, end-of-period, in percent

	Sep-07	Dec-07	Mar-08	Jun-08	Sep-08	Dec-08	Mar-09	Jun-09	Sep-09
China	4.4	4.5	4.1	4.5	3.8	2.8	3.2	3.2	3.5
Indonesia	9.2	10.0	11.7	13.4	13.2	11.9	12.7	11.1	10.0
Malaysia	3.7	4.1	3.8	4.9	4.6	3.2	3.8	4.4	4.2
Philippines	7.2	6.6	7.3	9.4	8.1	7.4	8.2	8.1	8.0
Thailand	4.7	5.0	4.6	5.9	4.4	2.7	3.3	3.7	4.0
Vietnam	8.6	9.1	9.2	16.0	15.0	10.2	9.5	9.7	10.3
Hong Kong, China	4.3	3.4	2.6	3.5	2.9	1.9	1.9	2.6	2.4
Korea, Rep. of	5.6	5.7	5.3	6.0	6.1	4.2	5.2	5.2	5.3
Singapore	2.7	2.7	2.3	3.6	3.2	2.1	2.0	2.6	2.5
Taiwan, China	2.6	2.6	2.4	2.7	2.2	1.4	1.5	1.6	1.4

Source: Bloomberg.

Foreign-Currency Government Bond Spreads (EMBIG), end-of-period, in basis points over U.S. Treasuries

	Sep-07	Dec-07	Mar-08	Jun-08	Sep-08	Dec-08	Mar-09	Jun-09	Sep-09
China	88	120	154	137	191	228	210	122	87
Indonesia	217	275	329	381	490	762	742	433	295
Malaysia	108	119	144	153	194	119	344	167	175
Philippines	184	172	207	303	324	546	432	324	265
Vietnam	156	203	283	368	404	747	574	379	290

Sources: JP Morgan, Bloomberg.

Credit Default Swap (CDS) Spreads on Foreign-Currency Government Bonds, 5-year, end-of-period, in basis points

	Sep-07	Dec-07	Mar-08	Jun-08	Sep-08	Dec-08	Mar-09	Jun-09	Sep-09
China	20	29	81	75	90	188	156	75	69
Indonesia	142	154	245	286	357	638	575	317	187
Malaysia	25	44	99	116	171	225	238	105	83
Philippines	145	153	243	266	284	384	360	217	176
Thailand	43	55	111	135	172	256	233	110	87
Hong Kong, China	9	18	58	42	62	104	145	68	56
Korea, Rep. of	24	47	97	107	182	319	328	182	101

Source: Thomson Datastream.

Appendix Table 12. Key Monetary Measures

	Capital injections	Liquidity Measures	Key policy rates	Deposit and Liabilities Guarantees
China	$19 billion to the state-owned Agricultural Bank of China	Cut the minimum required ratio (MRR) for large banks by 2% and for small banks by 3.5%. Reduce interest on excess reserves by 27 bps. Reduce rediscount rate by 252 bps. Scrap bank lending quotas. Started to use open market operations to fine tune monetary policy stance.	Cut one-year lending rate five times by a cumulative 216 bps.	
Indonesia		Cut MRR for FX deposits by 2 percentage points (from 3% to 1%) to provide more USD liquidity and allow use of central bank bills and government bonds as required reserves. Cut overnight repo rate by 200 basis points (from 12.25% to 10.25%). Increase overnight FASBI rate (return on commercial banks' short-term deposits with central bank) by 100 basis points (from 7.25% to 8.25%). Extend tenor of FX swaps from 7 days to 1 month. Extend open market operations (OMO) (tenor of non-regular OMO from 14 days to 3 months, tenor of FX swaps from 7 days to 1 year). Swap line with People's Bank of China: $18.5 billion, effective for 3 years. Swap line with Bank of Japan: $12 billion.	Cut base rate nine times by a cumulative 275 bps.	Guarantee deposits up to 2 billion rupiah ($205,000).
Malaysia		Cut the MRR by 3%. Swap line with People's Bank of China: $12 billion.	Cut the overnight policy rate three times by a cumulative 150 basis points.	Guarantee all deposits until December 2010.
Philippines		Cut MRR by 2%. Increased budget for peso rediscounting facility. Extend repo operations (wider range of collateral). Open new dollar deposit and new dollar repo facilities. Relax bank MTM rules on government bonds.	Cut the overnight reverse repo rate six times by a cumulative 200 bps.	
Thailand			Cut the one-day repo rate four times by 250 basis points.	Guarantee all deposits until August 2011.
Vietnam		Cut the MRR by 8%. Reduce discount rate by 700 basis points. Reduce refinancing rate by 700 basis points. Increase rates on reserve deposits by 140 basis points. Extend repo operations.	Cut the base rate six times by a cumulative 700 bps.	
Hong Kong, China	$2.6 billion to the Hong Kong Mortgage Corporation (for its revolving credit facility). Establish Contingent Bank Capital Facility (CBCF) to make available additional capital to locally-incorporated banks, until the end of 2010.	Temporarily expand discount window operations until March 2009 (wider range of collateral, tenor up to 3 months, higher threshold for the use of Exchange Fund paper). Extend market operations for direct liquidity assistance to banks (include foreign exchange swaps and term repos). Amend the lender of last resort (LOLR) framework (include securities in foreign currencies as eligible securities for repos and include foreign exchange swaps as an instrument for LOLR support). Swap line with People's Bank of China: $30 billion	Cut base rate thrice by a cumulative 525 bps.	Guarantee all deposits until the end of 2010.
Korea, Rep. of	$1.1 billion to the Korea Development Bank; $767 million to state-owned Industrial Bank of Korea; and, $729 million to the Korea EXIM Bank. Establish a bank recapitalization fund of $16 billion (amount drawn = $3.5 billion). Establish a toxic asset management fund of $34 billion (amount drawn = $563 million).	Extend OMO operations (wider range of collateral). Delay Basel II CAR rules by half year. Reduce rate on special SME loans by 75 basis points. Establish bond market stabilization fund of $8 billion. Swap line with U.S. Fed: $30 billion (amount withdrawn at the peak = $16.35 billion; balance remaining = $3 billion). Swap line with Bank of Japan: $30 billion. Swap line with People's Bank of China: $30 billion.	Cut 7-day repo rate six times by a cumulative 325 bps.	Guarantee $100 billion of borrowings by banks until the end of 2009.

Singapore	Open a Sukuk issuance facility and allow sukuk paper as eligible collateral for tapping central bank liquidity. Swap line with U.S. Fed: $30 billion.		Guarantee all deposits for three years.
Taiwan, China	Liquidity Injections: $3.6 billion. Cut the rate on accommodations with collateral and the rate on accommodations without collateral by 237.5 basis points each. Lowered the MRR. Allowed banks to use CDs, NCDs issued by the central bank, and redeposits with the central bank to borrow collateral loans. Extend repo operations (tenor of repos from 30 to 180 days, coverage of insurance companies). Raised the credit line for banks to extend funding to securities firms. Used $27.8 billion of foreign reserves as seed funds to participate in the foreign-currency call loan market.	Cut discount rate on 10-day loans seven times by a cumulative 237.5 bps.	Guarantee all deposits until the end of 2009. Guarantee interbank debt until the end of 2009. Raised the guarantee coverage on SME loans under the SME Credit Guarantee Fund.

Sources: National authorities, Reuters and World Bank staff.

Appendix Table 13. Key Measures in Fiscal Stimulus Packages

	Program Amount	Program Details and Status
China	$586 billion (12% of 2009 GDP)	• Transport, including rails, airports, and roads (RMB 1.5 trillion) • Post-earthquake reconstruction (RMB 1 trillion) • Public housing (RMB 400 billion) • Rural infrastructure, including electricity, water, and roads (RMB 370 billion) • Technological innovation (RMB 370 billion) • Energy and environment, including water sanitation, sewage, and restoration (RMB 210 billion) • Health care, education and cultural development (RMB 150 billion) (Note: stimulus package runs from 4Q 2008 to 2010)
Indonesia	$6.3 billion (1.3% of 2009 GDP)	• Tax cuts (IDR 43 trillion): Corporate income tax cut (IDR 18.5 trillion); Personal income tax cut (IDR 13.5 trillion); and, Increase in the income tax-free band (IDR 11 trillion). • Tax and imports duty subsidies for businesses and households (IDR 13.3 trillion): VAT on cooking oil and on oil and gas exploration (IDR 3.5 trillion); Import duties on raw materials and capital goods (IDR 2.5 trillion); Payroll tax (IDR 6.5 trillion); and, Geothermal tax (IDR 0.8 trillion). • Subsidies and budgetary expenditures (IDR 15 trillion): Price reductions on automotive diesel (IDR 2.8 trillion); Discounted electricity rates for industrial users (IDR 1.4 trillion); Additional infrastructure expenditures and government equity injections (IDR 10.6 trillion) --- IDR 1.7 trillion disbursed (15%); and, Community block grants (IDR 0.6 trillion).
Malaysia	First Package: $2 billion (0.9% of GDP)	• Low- and medium-cost housing (MYR 4.5 billion) • Micro-credit facilities (MYR 938 million) • Human development capital activities (MYR 1.4 million) • Disbursement rate for the first package is 61% as of end-September 2009.
	Second Package: $16.4 billion (9% of GDP)	• Tax cuts and incentives, including loss carry back for businesses, accelerated capital depreciation, and partial rebate of landing charges (MYR 3 billion) • Additional spending (MYR 15 billion), including for: school facilities (MYR 2 billion), investment promotion (MYR 1.6 billion), and infrastructure in Sabah and Sarawak (MYR 1.2 billion) • Guarantee funds (MYR 25 billion), including for: a working capital guarantee scheme (MYR 5 billion); a restructuring loan guarantee scheme (MYR 5 billion); and, for the establishment of a financial guarantee institution (MYR 15 billion). • Equity investments for the government-owned corporation Khazanah for investment in telecommunications, technology and tourism (MYR 10 billion) • Off-budget projects • "Private finance initiative" (MYR 2 billion) • Disbursement rate for the second package is 26% as of end-September 2009. (Note: Second package runs for a period of two years)
Philippines	$3.6 billion (1.8% of 2009 GDP)	• Corporate and individual tax breaks (PHP 40 billion) • Increase in the government budget (PHP160 billion) --- Allocations to Department of Agriculture, 67% disbursed; Department of Transportation, 11% disbursed; Department of Public Works, 36% disbursed; and, Department of Education, 50% disbursed. • Participation of government-owned and controlled corporations (GOCCs), government financial institutions (GFIs) and private sector in infrastructure projects (PHP 100 billion) --- Delayed to 2010. • Temporary additional benefits to members of social security institutions (GSIS, SSS and PHIL Health) (PHP 30 billion) --- PHP 10 billion of health benefits approved.

Thailand	First Package: $3.6 billion (1.1% of GDP)	• Tax cuts (THB 40 billion) • Cash transfers to 1.3 million civil servants and 8.1 million low-income social security fund beneficiaries (THB 19 billion) --- THB 17.9 billion disbursed as of end September 2009 (94%); Bus and rail travel and utility vouchers for low-income people (THB 11.4 billion) --- THB 11.3 billion disbursed (99%); and Commerce Ministry goods markets for low-income households (THB 1 billion) ---THB 628 million disbursed (63%). • Irrigation projects (THB 2 billion) --- THB 1.8 billion disbursed (89%); small reservoir construction projects for farmers (THB 0.8 billion) --- THB 420 million disbursed (55%); and, basic facilities works for villages (THB 1.5 billion) ---THB 1.4 billion disbursed (96%). • Food industry and SME promotion (THB 0.5 billion) --- THB 445 million disbursed (89%); tourism promotion (THB 1 billion) --- THB 642 million disbursed (64%), and national image rehabilitation THB 0.3 billion) --- THB 64 million disbursed (20%). • Subsidy for education of 10 million students (THB 19 billion) --- fully disbursed. • Training for about 240,000 unemployed workers (THB 6.9 billion) --- THB 2.7 billion disbursed (39%). • Economic Sufficiency Program (increased budget to 78,358 communities) (THB 15.2 billion) --- THB 5 billion disbursed (33%). • Subsidy for pensions of 5 million seniors (THB 9 billion) --- fully disbursed. • Subsidy for recruitment of 830,000 health volunteers (THB 3 billion) --- fully disbursed; and, improvement of 2,609 public health stations (THB1.1 billion) --- THB 776 million disbursed (71%). • Housing (construction of 532 residences) for junior police officers (THB 1.8 billion) --- THB 1.5 billion disbursed (82%). • Budgetary reserve for emergencies (THB 4.1 billion). • Transfers to government accounts (replenishment of Treasury reserves) (THB 19.1 billion) --- fully disbursed.
	Second Package: $45 billion (17.4% of GDP)	• Improve basic public services (THB 1.1 trillion): Transportation system and logistics (THB 676.3 billion); Energy security and alternative energy (THB 212.9 billion); public health infrastructure (THB 89.6 billion); Education infrastructure (THB 83.3 billion); Telecommunications network (THB 28.3 billion); Basic infrastructure to enhance welfare (THB 15.2 billion); Natural resources and environment infrastructure (THB 12.6 billion); and Science and technology infrastructure (THB 11.9 billion); infrastructure in support of tourism industry (THB 10.2 billion). • Improve efficiency of water distribution systems and small water reservoirs (THB 230.6 billion) • Generate more income and increased standard of living for the community and develop the southern border provinces (THB 100.1 billion). • Enhance quality of education (THB 60.1 billion). • Improve capacity building for the creative economy (THB 201. billion). • Enhance quality of public health (THB 9.3 billion). • Generate more income from tourism sector (THB 6.6 billion). • Of the package, projects approved in September for funding were: Irrigation and agriculture (THB 59 billion); Education (THB 44 billion); Transportation (THB 40 billion); Community spending (THB 32 billion); Health care (THB 12 billion); Social welfare (THB 7 billion); and, Others (THB 6 billion). Projects approved in October for funding were: Investment projects by local administrative and provincial organizations (THB 50.75 million); Agricultural product price guarantees (THB 40 billion); Capital injection for the Sufficient Community Project, Phase 2 (THB 19.56 billion); Capital injection to the Islamic Bank (THB 2.91 billion); Other projects requested by government agencies and SOEs (THB 27.03 billion); and Government petty cash allocations (THB 10 billion).
Vietnam	$3.7 billion (4% of 2009 GDP)	• Tax cuts (VND 20 trillion): Corporate income tax (VND 9.9 trillion); Personal income tax (VND 4.5 trillion); Value Added Tax (VND 4.5 trillion); and, Licenses and fees (VND 1.1 trillion). • Additional budgetary expenditures (VND 39.4 trillion): Budgetary advance from the 2010 budget (VND 18.2 trillion); Undisbursed funding in 2008 not to be returned to budget (VND 7.2 trillion); and, Investment funded by additional bond issuance (VND 14 trillion). • Additional lending by the Vietnam Development Bank (VND 7.1 trillion). • Interest rate subsidy program (not funded by the budget).

Korea, Rep. of	First Package: $53.1 billion (6.8% of 2009 GDP)	• Tax cuts (KRW 35.3 trillion) • Corporate and income tax cut (KRW 25.5 trillion) • Fuel and tariff tax cut (KRW 5.5 trillion) • Temporary investment tax reduction (KRW 3.0 trillion) • Tax benefit for long-term investment fund (KRW 1.3 trillion) • Tax rebates and subsidy for wage earners, self-employed, bus drivers, truckers, farmers, and fishermen (KRW 4.6 trillion) • Capital injection into state-owned banks (KRW 1.4 trillion) • Expenditure increase (KRW 10.0 trillion) • of which: • Infrastructure projects (KRW 4.0 trillion) • Support for SMEs (KRW 3.4 trillion) • Support for low-income families (KRW 1.0 trillion)
	Second Package: $12.6 billion (3.4% of GDP)	• Fiscal spending
	of which: $4.9 billion (0.8% of GDP)	• Emergency support program to support the poor: • Temporary public expenditure projects ($1.8 billion) • Temporary income support for the poor ($378 million) • Financial support for small businesses ($350 million) • Contribution to regional credit guarantee funds ($350 million) • Expansion of basic livelihood security programs ($205 million) • Financial support for the unemployed ($191 million)
Singapore	$13.6 billion (8% of 2009 GDP)	• Jobs credit scheme, skills program, workfare income supplement, and recruitment across the public sector (SGD 5.1 billion) • Enhanced bank lending schemes, bridging loan program, and risk-sharing schemes for trade financing (SGD 5.8 billion) • Tax concessions and measures to support business cash flow and to sharpen competitiveness (SGD 2.6 billion) • Direct assistance to households, targeted help for vulnerable groups, and support for charitable giving (SGD 2.6 billion) • Rejuvenation of public housing estates, upgrading of education and health infrastructure, and enhancement of sustainable development programs (SGD 4.4 billion)

Sources: National authorities, Reuters, and World Bank staff.

Appendix Chart 1. East Asia: Stock Market Price Indices

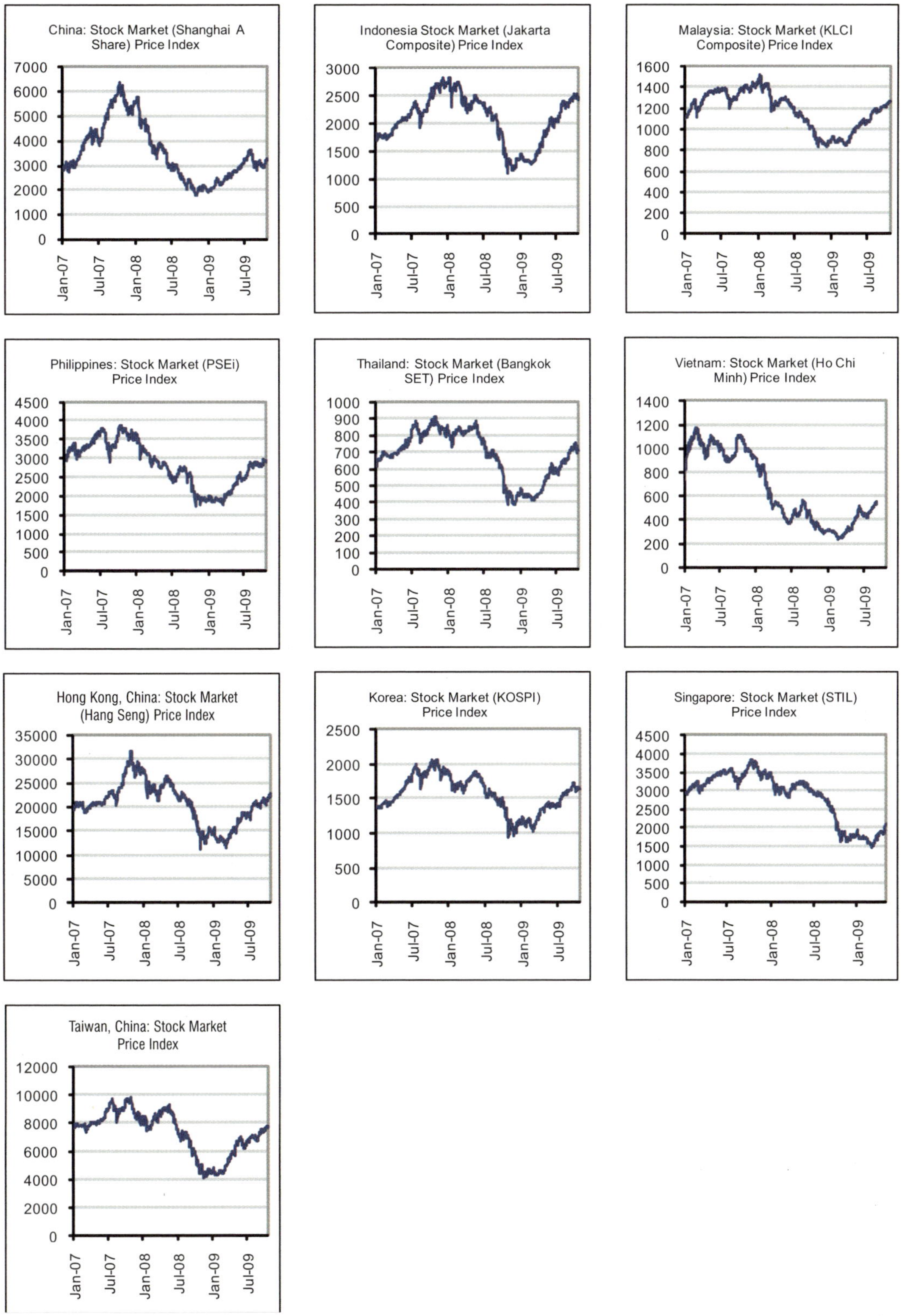

Appendix Chart 2. East Asia: Local-Currency 10-Year Government Bond Yields

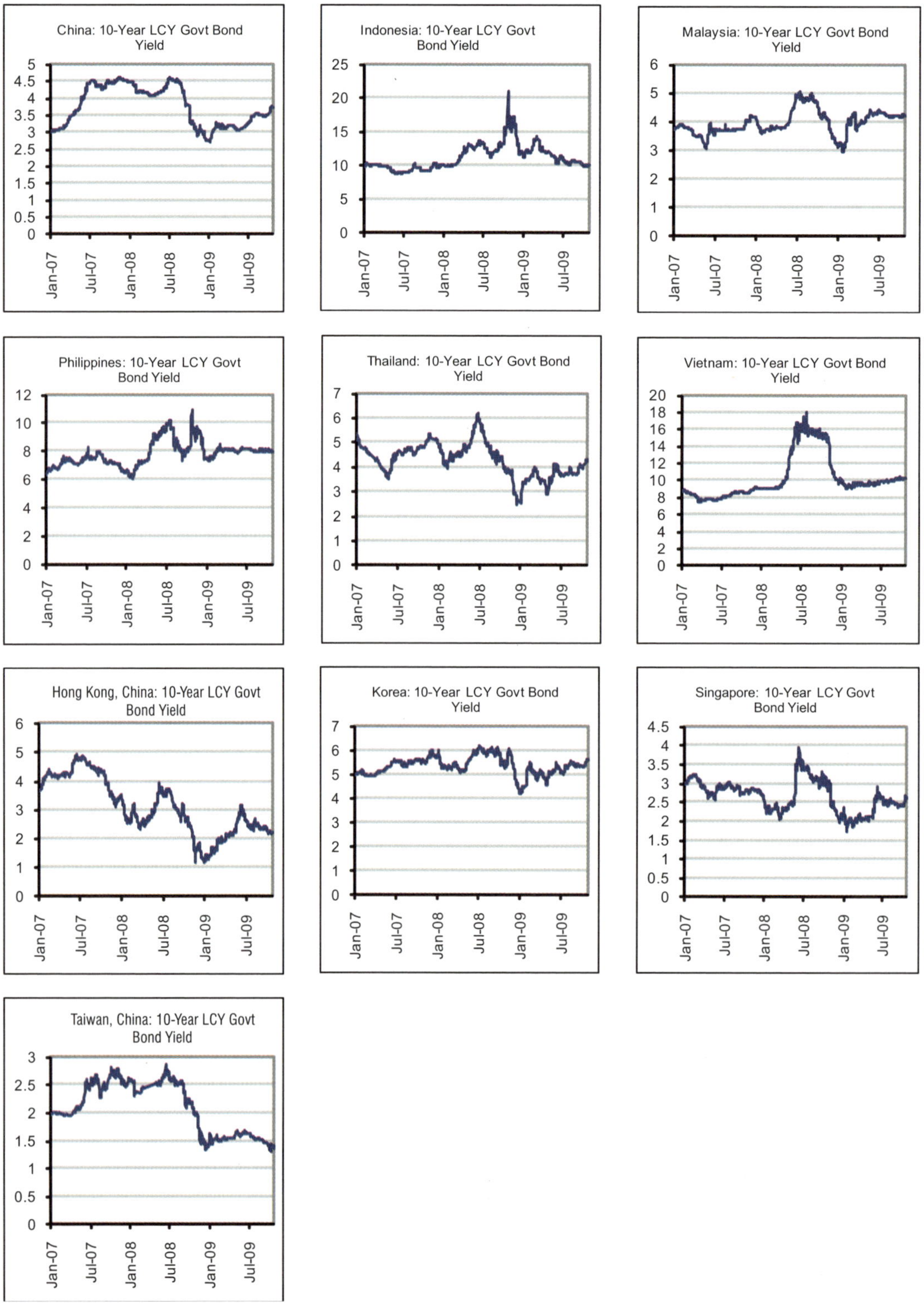

Appendix Chart 3. East Asia: Foreign-Currency Government Bond Spreads

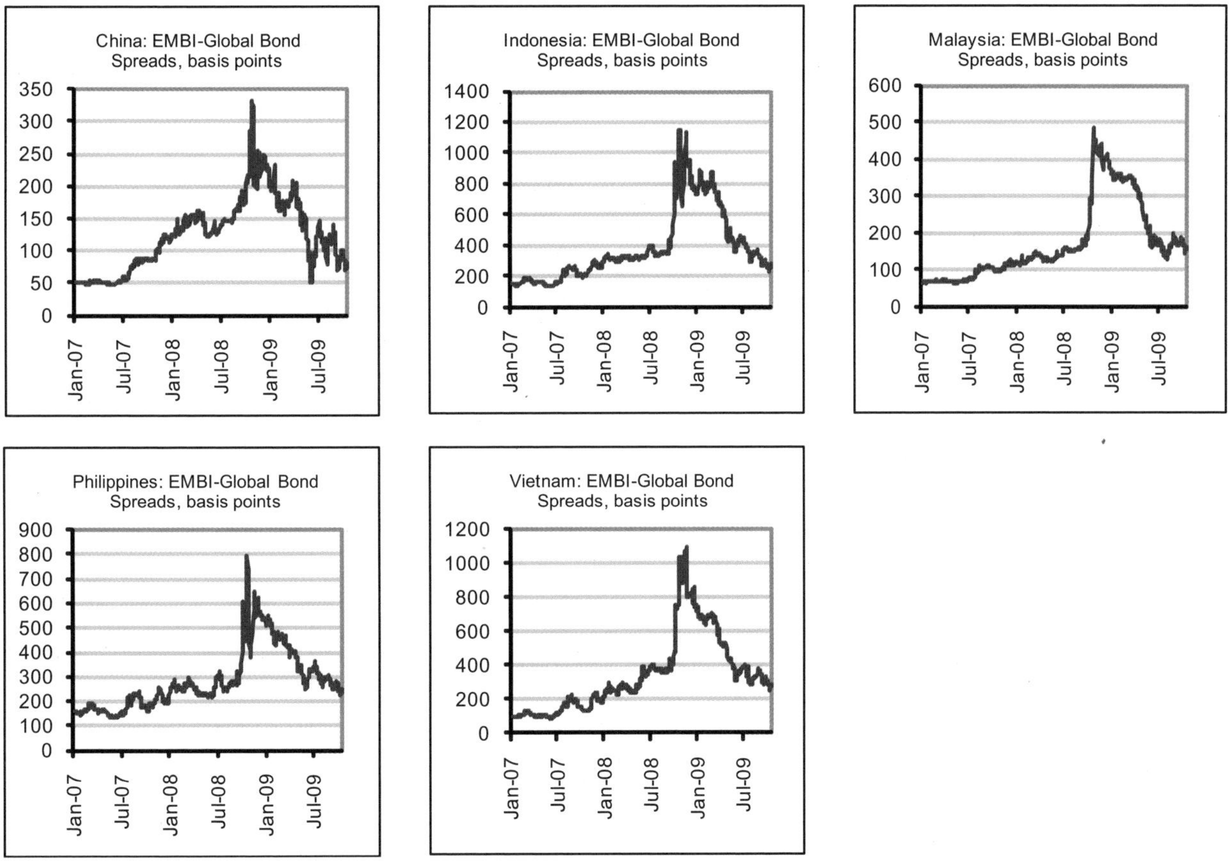

Source: JP Morgan Emerging Markets Bond Index Global (EMBIG), via Bloomberg.

Appendix Chart 4. East Asia: Sovereign Credit Default Swap (CDS) Spreads

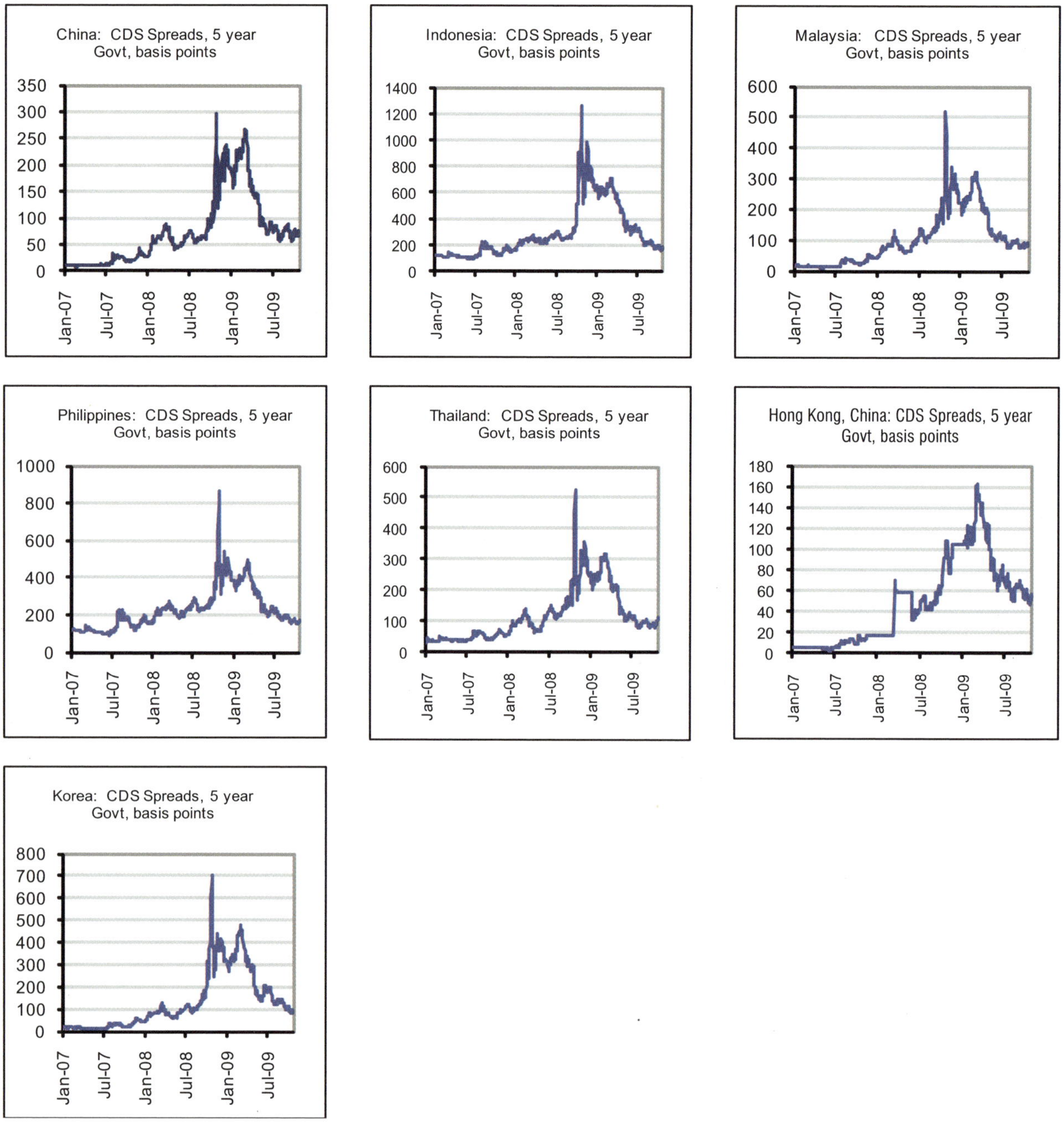